The Blood and The Glory

by Billye Brim

HARRISON HOUSE

Tulsa, Oklahoma

09 08 07 06 05   20 19 18 17 16 15

The Blood and The Glory
ISBN 1-57794-058-X
Copyright © 1995 by Billye Brim
P. O. Box 126
Collinsville, Oklahoma 74021

Published by Harrison House, Inc.
P. O. Box 35035
Tulsa, Oklahoma 74153

Contents

Introduction

Today's world contains many forces that, on the surface, seem out of our control. The recent national tragedy has threatened our sense of safety and security. How can we be safeguarded in a world where evil seems so prominent?

When the Lord directed me to write this book He impressed upon me that this was a necessary message for the church and her protection in the last days. As Christians, we are marked by a covering that no evil force can remove—the blood of Jesus. Under the protection of the blood we find a safe retreat. We can remain steadfast in a position of strength through the blood of Jesus Christ.

The last days are upon us and the world is becoming increasingly dangerous. However, protection for you and your family during this time is possible. By pleading the blood of Jesus over your property, possessions, and family, you can put worry to rest. For many these last days can be full of dread, fear, and insecurity. For the church they will be our best ever! Don't let terror defeat you. Discover how *The Blood and The Glory* will arm you and your family for war—both nationally and spiritually.

—Billye Brim

The Revelation of the Blood: How It Came

1

I was not looking for a revelation of the Blood when it came; I was looking for a manifestation of the Glory.

For I had been on a more than twenty-year-long Holy Spirit-led study of the Glory of God. The revelation of God's glory manifested in His church became the central theme of my ministry and the yearning of my heart.

The church the Lord Jesus Christ comes to receive unto Himself will not be a downtrodden, backslidden, weakened church, but will be filled with the glory of God. (Ephesians 5:27.)

I heard faithful men and women of God prophesy about it through those years. Reoccurring themes in the prophecies which so thrilled me spoke of signs, wonders, miracles, and even translations. I heard through the lips of more than one proven prophet that even the faces of believers will be so changed they will shine with the glory of God as His presence fills His temple.

Through these twenty years the Lord called me and caused me to witness prophecy-fulfilling world events. We began to travel and minister in the Soviet Union in 1980. The ministry has covered the gamut of running from the KGB down dark alleys and across railroad tracks to preaching openly in front of the former National Museum of Atheism after the collapse of communism. In 1986, after my husband moved to heaven, I studied Hebrew in Israel. Since then I return to the Land usually twice a year and have spent much time there in the unique doors God has opened to watch the fig tree (Israel) close at hand. Many of the miraculously returned Jews who are the sign of the soon return of the Lord are my close friends.

As a student of Bible prophecy, I saw signs in the nations, in the Jews, and in the church that now is the time. It is time for the glory of God to be poured out upon and manifested through the church.

And I was watching for it, closely, when I saw something else.

Satanic Attacks

I saw what seemed to be an increase in satanic attacks.

All were terrible. Some were inexplicable.

Strife struck between brethren who had preached the same message for years. Homes were broken when lives we thought were dedicated to the ministry of the Lord succumbed to sin and its consequences.

But the "inexplicable" cases especially drew me to seek an answer. No place-giving sin was involved. Innocent lives were lost to earth's realm when drunk drivers out of nowhere hit vehicles carrying God's faithful servants. Freak accidents in two cases struck the host ministry's families just before large meetings.

I sought the Lord about it.

He answered me with a question.

You preach about the last days and the signs of the times, do you not?

"Yes."

What did I tell you the devil would do in the last days?

I knew where to look. So I turned to Revelation 12:12 and read, "...The devil is come down unto you, having great wrath, because he knoweth that he hath but a short time."

In my Bible I had written in the margin that the Greek word translated "time" is *kairos* which means a limited and definite portion of time, a set time.

I thought first about the set time of Adam's lease.

After God finished His six-day workweek, He handed the authority on earth to Adam. Some Bible scholars believe God gave Adam a corresponding six-day lease to work upon earth, with a thousand years as a day. Adam, however, committed high treason and delivered his authority to Satan. He legally, but not morally, sub-let his domain to Satan who became the god of this world (Luke 4:6; 2 Corinthians 4:4). When the set time of Adam's lease is over, Satan will be evicted and sent to the pit.

Satan knows about time. When Jesus was on earth, demons asked Him, "...Art thou come hither to torment us before the time?" (Matthew 8:29).

The time. I saw it. This has to do with the time. Satan's lease is about up and he's furiously defying the prophecy of his doom.

Then I heard, *Back up a verse.*

So I read Revelation 12:11, "And they overcame him by the blood of the Lamb, and by the word of their testimony..."

The Blood! The Blood of Jesus!

Rushing in upon me came Holy Spirit guided thoughts concerning the Blood of Jesus and the primary weapon it is for the final hour of this age.

Remembering: Using the Name and the Blood To Bring Up Children 2

My thoughts traveled back to 1967 when I was baptized in the Holy Spirit.

For it was soon after that life-changing event that I first heard about using the Blood of Jesus to overcome the devil. Extreme hunger for the Word of God consumed me. In one of the seminars I attended I heard the minister say, "I always say it like this. I say, 'In the Name of Jesus, I plead the Blood of Jesus.' "

I remembered how those welcome words penetrated my heart as a young mother of four. And I remembered how we used them to bring up our children without tragedy.

Several incidents came to mind.

Chip, our youngest, could be described as "all boy" including almost everything that description usually brings to mind. Athletic. Fun loving. And so on. I was particularly thankful for the right to use the Blood of Jesus when Chip as a teen driver left the house in his car.

Things would transpire something like this. Chip, usually in a hurry to get to practice or a game or somewhere, would dutifully stand while I put my right hand on top of his curly black hair and said, "In the Name of Jesus, I apply the Blood of Jesus over Chip."

Sometimes I walked out to the car and put my hand on it, and sometimes I just added these words in the kitchen with my hand on his head, "In the Name of Jesus I apply the Blood of Jesus over Chip's car, bumper to bumper, side to side, top to bottom, every working part. Chip will go and come home safe."

Once this people-loving teenager invited several members of his high school football team to the house to cook hamburgers. As they prepared to leave, I decided not to embarrass Chip. I would wait till they left and then make my confession of God's provision in Jesus' Blood.

Chip got into his car loaded with friends, then got out of it and came back into the kitchen and asked in a somewhat demanding tone, "What kind of a mother are you? Are you going to let me go without the Blood of Jesus on me?"

Later, when he was in college an interesting thing happened. Chip and three friends decided to rent a house their second year rather than to live in the dorm.

Early one morning my telephone rang. At first I didn't recognize the high-pitched distorted voices.

"Mom!" "Mrs. Brim!" They squeaked excitedly.

I figured out it was Chip and his basketball player friend, Conley. They told me their scary story.

The doublewide mobile home they rented was far out in the country. The first day when the boys arrived home from school in one car, they noticed strange things. The doors and windows were open. Hair dryers and toasters were on. The television and stereos were blasting. They thought it was someone playing a joke. But when they checked with the owner, no one else had a key. For several days thereafter when they came home the same things were happening. And then came the eventful night before they called me.

Chip was in his bedroom studying. Everyone else was in bed. He heard the front door slam hard. The whole mobile home shook. He got up to investigate. Then the door to Conley's room opened wide and slammed closed.

Chip asked Matt, who slept on the living room couch, "Did you see that?"

"Yes. What was it?"

At that Conley's door opened and slammed again.

Then Chip and Matt saw a dark figure go out the front door which opened and slammed shut.

Matt and Chip ran to Chip's room where they both spent the rest of the night in his twin bed. They promised never to tell anyone what they saw.

Rising unusually early Conley said to Chip, "I've got to talk to you about last night."

(Conley and Chip grew up together. Conley's parents were Spirit-filled Christians, too. Chip told me when we discussed this for the book, however, that he and Conley were not living for God as they knew to at the time.)

Robert evidently had heard it too, for he asked, "What was all that?"

Conley said, "Something came into my room and stood over my bed. It was hooded and carried a scythe like the grim reaper. I think he came to tell me I'm going to die."

Matt cried out, "Oh, my God!"

With that the four boys took off running down the road toward a little store a mile away where they called me from the pay phone.

Such cases are low-level devils. They can only frighten. But this one had succeeded fairly well. For I am certain those macho athletic types would not have wanted the girls on campus to have observed their shaking and squeaking.

"It's just low-level devils," I assured them. I gave them Scriptures and told them how to cast out the devils.

Then I instructed them further. "Do you have any oil? Demons don't have to use windows and doors, but as a point of contact for your faith, and as a symbol of entry into your house, anoint all the doors and windows with this oil and say, 'In the Name of Jesus we apply the Blood of Jesus. Demons, you cannot enter our house.' "

The boys chipped in and bought oil at the store. Then they went back to the house—which they'd vowed on the way to the store they would never enter again—and carried out the instructions in detail.

They had no further trouble. And as a result of the evident power of God over the power of the devil, the boys started going to church.

Our older son, Terry, had a similar incident his senior year at Panhandle State University in far western Oklahoma. Terry and his friends were cowboys.

Terry had just rented a bedroom two days before from some other students to cut down on expenses. That night there had been a lot of alcohol, girls, and music. Terry who was not partying just went to bed.

About an hour later his room got very cold and dark. Slowly his twin bed with him in it rose about three feet off the floor.

These are his words as he described it to me for this book.

"I knew what it was. And I knew if I could say *Jesus* it would quit. But I felt literally paralyzed. I could have said anything but *Jesus*. It was like that part of my brain that could say *Jesus* was gone. But I kept trying. When I did get it out, the bed slowly came down."

Terry told a Christian professor he knew from the church he attended in Guymon. The teacher came in with him and they applied the Blood of Jesus over the mobile home. In the six months he had left to live there until graduation nothing like that happened again.

In teaching on the power in the Name of Jesus and the Blood of Jesus I have told this incident and asked how many have had a like experience. It seems to be rather common. But it is always the case—no matter what the demonic deception—that one can utter that Name and the devils have to flee as it is written. (Mark 16:17; James 4:7.)

While writing this book at home tonight, I telephoned both sons to get details of the accounts I've included. Both made similar statements to this effect: It was amazingly easy to stop the demon activity. And since seeing how easy it was, demons have not been able to so frighten them.

Both told me how they now use the Name of Jesus and the Blood of Jesus with their mouths morning and night over their families.

We recalled lots of other incidents.

Terry, who was a bull rider, remembered one close call when a gate failed to open properly and he was hung up in a chute with a violent bull. Someone who helped him get out said they didn't know how every bone in his body was not broken. Terry knew why.

We always used Psalm 34:19,20: "Many are the afflictions of the righteous: but the LORD delivereth him out of them all. He keepeth all his bones: not one of them is broken." With almost daily confession of this Scripture, we brought up four very active children—even our daughter, Brenda, played basketball—without one broken bone.

Chip recalled how we had him read Psalm 91 before every game.

And talking about how I used to plead the Blood over his car, he said, "I wouldn't be alive if you hadn't done that." I didn't push him for details because I really don't want to know.

Shelli, our oldest, is an anointed preacher and a singer. Brenda works in the administration of our ministry. They too are bringing up their boys and girls using the Blood of the Lamb and the Word of God.

Because of God's wonderful provision I know the joy of another Scripture. This is my own paraphrase, "I rejoice greatly that I find my children walking in truth..." (2 John 1:4.)

It makes much sense to me that when I sought the Lord about the increase in satanic attacks and He began to give me the illumination about His Blood, the first thing He brought to my mind concerned families and loved ones.

For I seemed to sense the heart cry of parents all over the world who are bringing up children in these trying times. I was conscious of the desperate cry of mothers in inner cities, "What can I do? This neighborhood. The drugs. The gangs. How can I keep my child alive?"

I seemed to know they were crying out for knowledge of the power in the Blood of Jesus to overcome Satan and his demons.

The illumination I would be led into of the use of the power in the Blood of Jesus would surpass anything I had known and was to be shared with others. Hence this book.

Later we shall examine in detail the scriptural basis for pleading, or applying, the Blood of Jesus. We shall see that one can draw a Blood line around loved ones and possessions.

But now, for the next step God took me down on this road of revelation concerning the powerful weapon of the Blood of Jesus in overcoming the devil.

The Old-Timers: And the Truth They Knew

3

The next step eventually led to a bright light in the Word of God. When I saw it, it illuminated me concerning my questions: "How is the enemy able to 'come out of the blue' so to speak in attacks against faithful Christians? And how can we prevent them?"

First, a statement in Dr. Kenneth E. Hagin's book, *The Triumphant Church*,[1] struck me deeply.

He gave an account of how a missionary in the early part of this century overcame the always deadly sting of a venomous scorpion by saying, "I plead the Blood of the Lord Jesus Christ against this scorpion sting." The natives watched the woman expecting her to die. When she suffered no ill effects most of them accepted Jesus.

In relating this Dr. Hagin commented, "Every benefit and blessing we possess in our redemption, including complete and total victory over Satan, is based on Jesus and His triumph over Satan at the Cross. We have victory over Satan because of Jesus' shed Blood. The old-timers in Pentecost understood a truth about the Blood of Jesus. They would plead the Blood against the devil. That's scriptural."

Those last three sentences leaped from the page and lodged in my heart. And from deep within me sprang up, what I believe to be, a God-given desire to know what the old-timers understood about the Blood of Jesus.

Almost immediately thereafter someone just handed me Mrs. C. Nuzum's book, *The Life of Faith*.[2] I remembered at once this was the first book Kenneth Hagin read about faith after he came off the deathbed through faith in God. It was first published in 1928 and Mrs. Nuzum was at least 71 at the time so she qualified as an old-timer.

Faith in the Blood

Mrs. Nuzum's clear communication of her effectual faith fed my own. But it was especially her faith in and use of the Blood of Jesus which answered both the desires and questions of my heart.

Mrs. Nuzum, a missionary to Mexico, "was born sick" according to the words of her testimony.[3] She described herself throughout childhood and young womanhood as crippled with rheumatism, paralyzed on the left side, suffering heart problems, and given up by the best doctors to die—until she received divine healing.

"For 27 years," she says, "I was never free from pain...But now at the age of 71, I am doing the work of three women and have not lain in bed from sickness for so long that I cannot remember when I did so last."

She considered all the evil that can come to us as from the devil, directly or indirectly.[4] But she clearly believed and demonstrated, "God is not willing that we should be overcome even once, (He) *'always* causeth us to triumph in Christ'—not one failure as we obey and trust."[5]

> God has given us a wonderful weapon to use, the blood of Jesus. This is our weapon, our shield, our hiding place...
>
> In Revelation 12:11 we are told that, "They overcame him by the blood of the Lamb, and by the word of their testimony." Sin, temptation, sickness, disease, everything that comes from Satan is included in that. The Blood overcame *him*. When anything is overcome it has no more power. This Book says they overcame him by the blood of the Lamb and by the word of their testimony. Not merely by your word or their word, but by your testimony to what God has done coupled with your faith in the Blood is the overcoming accomplished. No matter in what way the enemy comes, whether in discouragement, temptation, sickness, or any other way, he is overcome by the blood of the Lamb, and by the word of our testimony.[6]

Mrs. Nuzum proved her weapons. Notice how the challenges she faced match any of the present day.

I want to give you some instances showing that God does really stand by His promises concerning the Blood.

I was down in Mexico when so many bandits were active, and at one time was in a town when the United States authorities sent us word to get out, that we were in great danger, the red-flaggers were coming. The Mexican authorities also sent us word to get out. Nearly all the families went away and they asked me to go, but God did not give me any liberty to go, although the authorities did not promise me any protection. However, I told them I was not looking to them to take care of me, but was trusting God; and, as He was taking care of me, I was just as safe surrounded by those marauders as when alone.

One day I heard a noise and looking out, I saw...soldiers coming. I never thought of danger, although the road ran very close to my door. I went and stood in the doorway to look in their faces and see what they were like (I tell this to show how God had taken the fear away). I was in a large adobe house all alone with God, and I went to bed and slept sweetly all night. These soldiers were in the town two days and nights, and usually they took the largest house in town (I was in the largest), but they entered every house except mine, and did not come into my house at all...

This Blood avails for all things; it is our protection against everything if we will cry for it and trust in it. At one time I walked to a town about six miles distant, as the mules and horses were all away. On my way back I was some distance from any house, when I saw a company of men sitting and drinking muscale (...whiskey), and I saw they were becoming quite drunk with it. I left the path and circled around, but perceiving one of them had seen me and was coming after me as fast as he could, and was rapidly gaining on me at every step; I saw my danger and cried out for the Blood to protect me from this drunken man. Almost immediately his attention was attracted by some little thing along the road and he seemed to forget all about me...

One day I was starting to go into a house, and just as I stepped inside the gate, there was a terrible ferocious bulldog. I held my umbrella in front of me but he broke it in an instant; then he grabbed me close to the knee, holding my limb between his teeth. I cried for the protection of the Blood, and that dog could not shut his jaws. The people in the house were greatly surprised that I was not torn to pieces...

I went into a house one day and found the whole family down with a fever similar to yellow fever; it is very dangerous. No one would come to help them because they were afraid of it. I felt that I could not leave them that way, so I cried out for the protection of the Blood and stayed with them all that day and night, going from one bed to another waiting on them. I never had a sign of the fever.

Even death has to recede before this precious Blood of Jesus. A woman in Douglas had consumption. Her husband was a railroad man and friends telegraphed him that his wife was dying. In their house was a friend who believed in Divine Healing and she sent for me. We had prayer and the woman was better, but the devil came in an onslaught. When I went back my friend said she had a sort of vision and everything in the room was black, except herself and me, and we were like two white specks. She said, "I know death has struck her," and I saw that her face was ashy. I just bent over her and pleaded the power of the Blood of Jesus

Christ. After a while she drew a long breath, opened her eyes and said: "It is gone." Surely, death had fled before the mighty Name and the Blood of Jesus Christ. She is a well woman today.

I do not believe we half know the gift Jesus Christ gave us when He gave us this Blood.[7]

I found in Mrs. Nuzum's book—as well as in the accounts of many other old-timers affected by the outpouring of the Spirit at the beginning of the Twentieth Century—much emphasis on the Blood. It was upon their lips in prayer, practical use, sermon, and song. Many of our songs about the Blood come from that time.

This might be a good place to insert something else the Lord spoke to me about the Blood. He showed me that Satan has systematically tried to rob from the church, truth about the Blood of Jesus and its practical use. Especially as a primary weapon against him.

He called to my remembrance how some years ago a major denomination took all the Blood songs out of their hymnals, with a resultant loss of power. They said the Blood frightened little children.

Little children are not frightened by the joyous singing of, "There is power, power; Wonder-working power, In the Blood, of the Lamb."

But someone is. Satan is.

Then the Lord impressed me, *You* (the Word or Charismatic churches I usually speak in) *do not have song books. You have overhead projectors. But what is the difference in their removing the Blood songs from their hymn books and your removing them from your repertoires?*

So I began to take a survey. I paid close attention when I went to our churches. Much more often than not the song service did not include one song about the Blood. (And consider that it is through the Blood we have access.) The preaching usually did not contain mention of the Blood. I believe this is changing now, however, for it must.

One old-timer, Carl Roos, told me before he moved to heaven, "The Lord told us, 'Make much of the Blood; and the Blood will make much of you.'"

That concept of "honoring the Blood of Jesus" was well known to the saints I have researched. Like Mrs. Nuzum they had faith in the power of the Blood. And they wielded their weapon. Often by setting a watch with it—a Blood watch.

The Price of Constant Victory

It was in this area that I found the answer I was seeking. The preventative action we can take against Satan's unfair blows.

In Mrs. Nuzum's book in Chapter Seven entitled, "Hold Fast That Which Thou Hast" she exposed the doors Satan uses to enter and "take a place."

> We are all in the land of the enemy and are subject to his attacks in spirit, soul, and body, but God says, "Give no place to the devil" (Ephesians 4:27). That means that he cannot take a place in us when he attacks us if we do not *let him*. We open the way for him to come in if we sin; the smallest sin we commit in word, deed, or thought, gives place for the devil to do us harm.[8]

The first door she mentioned is obvious—sin.

Thank God for the Blood of Jesus which cleanses us from all sin and makes us new creations when we are born again.

And thank God, if we sin after we are born again, we can take advantage of First John 1:9: "If we confess our sins, he is faithful and just to forgive us our sins, and cleanse us from all unrighteousness."

It is the Blood in either case which cleanses us and closes the door of opportunity to the devil.

But when I read what she had to say about another door—I knew I had what I was looking for—an opening Satan uses to afflict the innocents, and how to keep it closed.

God's remedy always accomplishes just what God says it will accomplish—overcome the enemy. But watchfulness is the price of constant victory. "Be vigilant (watch all the time) because your adversary the devil as a roaring lion walketh about, seeking whom he may devour" (1 Peter 5:8).

Our enemy is so set on our destruction that he never sleeps, or neglects to follow after us to destroy us. How sad that we, who have so much at stake, should be less diligent than he. A failure to watch, also gives the devil a place in us or permits him to return. "I say unto all, Watch." We are not safe from his attacks one moment, without the Blood of Jesus. As soon as we waken in the morning we should cry for the Blood to be upon us, within us, around us, and between us and all evil and the author of evil. The last thing before we sleep we should, in the same way, cry for the protection of the Blood...

Oh, that we could rouse ourselves to a greater intensity in the things of God. We are so halfhearted and yet we must overcome an enemy that is constantly alert and ready to take advantage of all carelessness and neglect. Soldiers are severely dealt with for even a small carelessness or neglect. If we neglect to watch, can God call us good soldiers? Oh, how much we suffer because we fail to watch all the time. "I say unto *all*, Watch." Not one person is excused from watching. We shall never in this life get to a place where the enemy cannot attack us, but God is not willing that we should be overcome even once, "*always* causeth us to triumph in Christ"—not one failure as we obey and trust.[9]

I saw it! First Peter 5:8 is so clear! Be vigilant! Watch!

That's how he slips in on us! A lack of watchfulness!

The old-timers set up a watch. A Word watch. A Blood watch. They drew a Blood line Satan could not cross.

But can you do it?

What is the scriptural basis?

I had to go back. All the way back. Back to the plan of God. Back to the glory. Back before the foundation of the world.

---

[1]Kenneth E. Hagin, *The Triumphant Church* (Kenneth Hagin Ministries, Box 50126, Tulsa, OK 74150), 187, 188.

[2]Mrs. C. Nuzum, *The Life of Faith* (Gospel Publishing House, Springfield, MO 65802).

[3]Ibid., 11-13.

[4]Ibid., 37, 60.

[5]Ibid., 39.

[6]Ibid., 50, 54.

[7]Ibid., 56-59.

[8]Ibid., 37.

[9]Ibid., 38, 39.

The Revelation of the Glory: How It Came

4

L ife in the early '70s was busy and happy for me. At home I was a wife and mother of four. At work I was editor of publications for a minister who had been charged by the Lord to put all his teachings into printed form. My job was to help him do that by editing them into a magazine and books which now have reached around the globe in multiplied millions.

My childhood call to the ministry knew its real beginning—though I did not recognize it as such until years later—when the eight or so members of the adult Sunday School class of the Friends (Quaker) church elected me teacher in about 1973.

Every Sunday I taught the good Word of God I'd learned in the lessons I had edited the previous week. And in the move of the Spirit so thrilling in those days, the class grew from eight to two hundred and moved from the choir loft to fill the auditorium.

The minister I worked for based his ministry on the written Word of God and being led by the Spirit of God. He walked with the Lord in close, personal fellowship and aimed to conduct the ministry in obedience to the Lord's leadings.

About this time he was impressed of the Lord that it would behoove him to study all the Scriptures on "the glory." He did so. And from time to time as the Lord led, he preached on "The Glory of God."

He usually began the message by simply reading the Scriptures which describe God's glory in manifestation from the Old Testament through the New. Often an unusual presence of God would accompany this special sermon. Sometimes the glory of God took the form of a bright cloud as in the Old Testament. Like a wave it would roll across the congregation. Signs and wonders would follow as God confirmed His Word.

Inspired by the evidently supernatural touch upon this subject, and led by the Spirit I am sure, I received a thought that affected the rest of my life and ministry.

If it would behoove him to study these Scriptures, it would behoove me.

So I determined to study the glory. About the same time I made another decision. Our rapidly growing Sunday School class included many new believers unfamiliar with the overall plan of God. So I decided to begin at Genesis and take an overview of God's plan of redemption. The two studies so merged that I came to see the Bible as "The Story of the Glory."

For a few years, I experienced a most wonderful Holy Spirit guided course of learning. It was even interspersed with vision which brought precious insight into the glory of His plan.

My now twenty-year-long study of, meditation on, preaching about, yearning and watching for, "The Glory of God" is condensed and offered here because it fits. The Blood and the Glory go together in God's wonderful plan of redemption.

Oh! What a Planner! Oh! What a Plan!

The World That Then Was

5

From the start of our Sunday School class journey beginning at the beginnings, light shined upon questions I'd had since childhood but was afraid to ask.

Why did God make the devil, anyway? Didn't He know he was going to cause me all this trouble?

How old is earth? How long has man lived on it?

Is science right? Are the preachers right?

While I would not be dogmatic about some of these things, they enlightened me as to our ability always to triumph in Christ Jesus over the enemy.

GENESIS 1:1

1 In the beginning God created the heaven and the earth.

Only God could sum up so much in so few words. For everything the Bible's opening verse includes would fill volumes the world could not contain.

What it does not include is verse two.

GENESIS 1:2

2 And the earth was without form, and void; and darkness was upon the face of the deep....

God did not create the earth "without form and void." That state of things came later. The original language of the Bible reveals this to us.

The Hebrew words translated "without form and void" are the rhyming words *tohu va' bohu*. (Pronounced phonetically: toe'-who vah bow'-who.)

A Hebrew English lexicon defines them as: *Tohu*: formlessness, confusion, unreality, emptiness, chaos, waste. *Bohu*: emptiness. *Va* simply means "and".[1]

When I taught along these lines at a Bible School in Munich, a German woman helped me with the definition of this phrase. Her eyes lit up with understanding when I said the Hebrew words.

"We know what *tohu v'bohu* means," she spoke out loudly. "We use that saying. We got it from the Jews. It's like this. You cleaned your house perfectly. It is spotless. Then you walk down the hall and open the door to your teenager's room. You scream, 'This place is *tohu v'bohu!* Clean it at once!'"

God did not create earth a formless, confused, empty, chaotic mess. Such a creation would not meet the biblical criteria for God's work.

God's work is perfect (Deuteronomy 32:4).

God's work is glorious (Psalm 111:3).

The Bible provides its own commentary on *tohu v'bohu*. We will examine two passages which give further revelation to the first two verses of the Bible.

The first specifically states that God did not make earth *tohu*.

ISAIAH 45:18

18 For thus saith the LORD that created the heavens; God himself that formed the earth and made it; he hath established it, he created it not in vain (*tohu*), he formed it to be inhabited: I *am* the LORD; and *there* is none else.

God created earth in a state of glorious perfection.

Planet earth fell into the chaotic ruin described in the Bible's second verse.

The Hebrew word translated "was" in Genesis 1:2 is very enlightening. The Lexicon gives the basic meaning of this verb as *fall out, come to pass, become, be*. Further definition includes *happen, occur, come to pass*.[2]

With the meaning of *so it came to pass*, the *King James* translates the same word "and it was so" in Genesis 1:7,9,11,15,24,30.

In many places the *King James Version* translates this word, "And it came to pass...." Genesis 12:14 is one of them.

The first two verses of the Bible can be translated as well :

1. In the beginning God created the heavens and the earth.

2. And the earth became without form, and void (*tohu v' bohu*) and darkness was upon the face of the deep....

E. W. Bullinger's comments in *The Companion Bible* state it like this: Not created *tohu* (Isaiah 45:18), but became *tohu* (Genesis 1:2, 2 Peter 3:5,6).[3]

Something catastrophic happened between the first and second verses of Genesis. Millions, perhaps billions, of years lie between them.

Someone has said, "As long as true science requires...."

God created Adam around 6000 years ago. But Earth is much older. Science now estimates it to be more than four billion years old.

The Day the Dinosaurs Died?

Bullinger's note on Genesis 1:1 reads: "The World That Then Was" (2 Peter 3:5,6). Creation in eternity past, to which all Fossils and 'Remains' belong.[4]

Earth we are told was habitable when God created it (Isaiah 45:18).

Dinosaurs may have been part of the "the world that then was." We know they were here long, long ago.

A big question among scientists is, "What happened to the dinosaurs?"

A wide range of theories—some of them quite funny—were put forth to answer this question. But recently many scientists have agreed on a theory that the last of the dinosaurs died on one cataclysmic day. They believe that a widespread mass extinction of animal life occurred when an asteroid collided with earth.

It is possible they are coming closer to the truth in that they realize there was indeed one catastrophic day.

I believe it was the day Lucifer fell.

For the Word of God gives us another passage using *tohu v'bohu*. Any good reference Bible has a mark next to "without form, and void" in Genesis 1:2 which refers to Jeremiah 4:23.

JEREMIAH 4:23-27

23 I beheld the earth, and, lo, *it was* without form, and void (*tohu v' bohu*); and the heavens, and they *had* no light.

24 I beheld the mountains, and, lo, they trembled, and all the hills moved lightly.

25 I beheld, and, lo, *there was* no man, and all the birds of the heavens were fled.

26 I beheld, and, lo, the fruitful place *was* a wilderness, and all the cities thereof were broken down at the presence of the LORD, *and* by his fierce anger.

27 For thus hath the LORD said, The whole land shall be desolate; yet will I not make a full end.

God caused Jeremiah to look into the past and see the day when judgment fell on "the world that then was" and earth became *tohu v'bohu*.... For the prophet clearly describes a horrifying day when:

Light was removed. God removed earth's light; Not just its natural light. God is Light (1 John 1:5).

Life was nowhere to be found. Even the birds were gone. Of course, when God removed the Light of Life every creature died in an instant.

Mountains and hills shook. I've wondered if this could have been when fault lines first occurred.

All the cities were destroyed. All—not some. Evidently the "world that then was" had cities. Via God's supernatural system which far surpasses telecommunications of today, the prophet watched a "replay" of their violent destruction.

What caused such total devastation?

"The presence of the LORD, by His fierce anger" (v. 26).

John G. Lake said, "The presence of God is as destructive of evil as it is creative of good."

The Fall of Lucifer

What made God so angry?

A rebellion so great it split the angelic hosts. A revolt against God led by the most beautiful being God had created, the archangel, Lucifer. The following passage describes him in the beauty of his creation.

EZEKIEL 28:12-15

12 ...Thou sealest up the sum, full of wisdom, and perfect in beauty.

13 Thou hast been in Eden the garden of God; every precious stone was thy covering, the sardius, topaz, and the diamond, the beryl, the onyx, and the jasper, the sapphire, the emerald, and the carbuncle, and gold; the workmanship of thy tabrets and of thy pipes was prepared in thee in the day that thou wast created.

14 Thou *art* the anointed cherub that covereth; and I have set thee so: thou wast upon the holy mountain of God; thou hast walked up and down in the midst of the stones of fire.

15 Thou *wast* perfect in thy ways from the day that thou wast created, till iniquity was found in thee.

Where did the iniquity originate?

To meet the criteria for God's handiwork—perfect and glorious—the beings He designed to work with Him must contain a certain "thing." That "thing" is dangerous to the Creator. But His created beings would be nothing more than puppets without it. That "thing" is a free will.

God is not a creator of Pinnochios or even of marvelous looking humanoid creatures programmed by microchips to worship and obey Him without fail. Indeed worship is only meaningful when the worshipper wills to worship. Obedience can bring God pleasure only when the "obeyer" chooses to obey.

One's will is his "chooser." With it he makes the choices which determine his eternal destiny.

God gave Lucifer—as He gave all the angels—a free will in the day of his creation. He must have used it to worship and please God for some measure of eternity. How long the Bible does not reveal. But it does reveal that he was the first to turn his will against the Father's and it caused his fall.

How did he fall? How did it happen? The following passage begins with those questions apparently asked by the kings of nations whom Satan deceived (Isaiah 14:9,10). And it supplies the answer.

ISAIAH 14:12-14

12 How art thou fallen from heaven, O Lucifer, son of the morning! *how* art thou cut down to the ground, which didst weaken the nations!

13 For thou hast said in thine heart, I will ascend into heaven, I will exalt my throne above the stars of God: I will sit also upon the mount of the congregation, in the sides of the north:

14 I will ascend above the heights of the clouds; I will be like the most High.

Lucifer's five treasonous "I wills" reveal much.

"I will ascend into heaven." His kingdom was in a place from which he had to go up to carry out his rebellious plan.

"I will exalt my throne above the stars of God." Lucifer had a throne, and therefore a kingdom.

"I will sit also upon the mount of the congregation, in the sides of the north." This describes the place of God's throne. Lucifer was after the throne of God.

"I will ascend above the heights of the clouds." The atmosphere of Lucifer's kingdom included clouds—clouds he would surmount in an attempt to exalt his throne. Many Bible scholars agree that his kingdom was here on earth. It was "the world that then was."

"I will be like the most High." All this entails we do not know. But his later temptation of Jesus reveals that he wanted to receive rather than to give worship.

There was a real "star wars"!

Lucifer deceived even some of the angels and led an organized revolt against the Most High God.

What was the outcome?

Jesus told us. "And he said unto them, I beheld Satan as lightning fall from heaven" (Luke 10:18).

I believe Lucifer's rebellion so angered God that He removed Himself from the environs of earth sending it into a chaotic wasteland covered with dark waters.

---

[1]Francis Brown, *A Hebrew and English Lexicon of the Old Testament*, Based on the Lexicon of William Gesenius (Oxford University Press, Oxford, London, New York), 1062, 96.
[2]Ibid., 224, 225.
[3]*The Companion Bible* (Kregal Publications, Grand Rapids, MI 49501) 3.
[4]Ibid., 3.

Circle of Glory

6

Throughout the intervening span of time between the Bible's first and second verses, earth lay beneath dismal waters in stark contrast to the glorious perfection of the rest of creation.

What did the angels think about the one dark spot in God's otherwise perfect order of things?

Did they just ignore it?

Did they talk about it?

I mention the angels because the Holy Spirit brought them to my attention as He taught me about the glory. He showed me they were watching when things began to change.

GENESIS 1:2

...And the Spirit of God moved upon the face of the waters.

Did the angels spread the news?

Did they say, "Something's going on there! The Holy Spirit is moving upon the dark spot!"?

They heard God's first words and watched their glorious fulfillment.

GENESIS 1:3

3 And God said, "Let there be light:" and there was light.

God was not commanding the sun and the moon to become. They didn't come forth until the fourth day. God was talking about the Light of Himself.

In essence this included: God is returning Light and Life to earth. He removed His Presence, but now He will work there again.

In God's work week He established a new order of things. He separated the waters. He called forth the seed that was in the earth; He did not create new plant life (vv. 11,12). He set the sun, the moon, the stars. He created new animal life (vv. 20,21).

His work progressed in divisions He called: The first day... The second day... The third day... The fourth day... The fifth day...

And then the sixth day! The most angel-astonishing day of all!

I heard His Voice within my spirit when He spoke to me about the sixth day.

I did not do this in a corner. All were watching when I stepped to center stage and made a declaration which rocked all creation as it reverberated from the regions of glory to the regions of the damned.

The words of Genesis 1:26 took on a new tone. My heart could hear it in loud, deliberate words as they may have been called out across the wide expanses of creation.

> *Let us make man in our image,*
> *after our likeness:*
> *and let them have dominion*
> *over the fish of the sea,*
> *and over the fowl of the air,*
> *and over the cattle,*
> *and over all the earth,*
> *and over every creeping thing that creepeth upon the earth.*

"What is a man?" "What is a man?" "What is a man?"

Angelic questions may have resounded in response to the startling news.

For one angel even dared to ask the Creator, we are told. Psalm Eight records his questions. We know these are the words of an angel; the New Testament tells us so (Hebrews 2:5-7).

A few commentators say this was Satan. I don't think so. I believe he may have been more of a Peter type angel daring to ask what others were wondering. Or perhaps the angel was led to articulate the questions for our enlightenment. In whatever way it occurred, God chose to record the angelic inquiry in His Holy Word.

PSALM 8:3-6

3 When I consider thy heavens, the work of thy fingers, the moon and the stars, which thou hast ordained;

4 What is man, that thou art mindful of him? and the son of man, that thou visitest him?

5 For thou hast made him a little lower than the angels (*Elohim*), and hast crowned him with glory and honour.

6 Thou madest him to have dominion over the works of thy hands; thou hast put all things under his feet:

Let us examine this in modern vernacular.

When I consider thy heavens, the work of thy fingers, the moon and the stars, which thou hast ordained.... This angel just had watched the wonders of the work of God in creation. So he began by complementing the Creator. Then he asked the big question.

What is man, that thou art mindful of him?

"What is a man? What is this being, O Creator, that he has a place in Your mind?"

And the son of man, that thou visitest him?

Angels may have had to call on God. Here is one whom God visits in the garden.

For thou hast made him a little lower than the angels (Elohim)....

The Hebrew word is not *angels*. It is *Elohim. Elohim* is the plural word for God. It shows God the Father, God the Son, and God the Holy Spirit. For eternity past the angels had known this order: The Triune Godhead, archangels, and angels. Now there is a new order in creation. Man is ranked just under the Godhead. The angels didn't even know the position was open.

Thou...hast crowned him....

Wonder of wonders to the amazed angel! God crowned man! He didn't ask Gabriel or Michael to do it. Amid majesty and pageantry far surpassing any crowning of any earthly monarch, God Himself arose and crowned His man.

Who wears crowns?

Kings. By this crowning God fixed forever the place of man in God's heart and in God's plans.

What was the crown made of? Of diamonds? Of gold?

No. God paves streets with gold. The crown was made of the most valuable substance in all creation.

Thou...hast crowned him with glory and honour.

The crown was made of glory! God's glory! Glory, which may seem abstract to some, is highest heavenly reality. For the glory of God is God's Presence manifested. The glory of God is God Himself.

God's glory sat upon man as his crown and clothed him as his covering. It fitted man for the fellowship he enjoyed with his Creator.

The Fall of Man

God's Word had gone forth: Man would have dominion over the works of God's hands.

Satan challenged it. If he could stop God's Word from coming to pass, he could defeat God.

His tactics were simple. He tempted the will of man. Man yielded and turned his will crosswise to the will of God.

Some of—*if not the*—saddest words in the Bible are:

GENESIS 3:8-10

8 And they heard the voice of the LORD God walking in the garden in the cool of the day: and Adam and his wife hid themselves from the presence of the LORD God amongst the trees of the garden.

9 And the LORD God called unto Adam, and said unto him, Where art thou?

10 And he said, I heard thy voice in the garden, and I was afraid, because I was naked; and I hid myself.

Early one Sunday morning I was meditating on these things in preparation for the class. I'd put on a roast for dinner. And I was fixing my hair in front of the wide mirror in our only bathroom before waking the family.

From behind me, high and to the right, I heard a Voice. It probably was not audible—but to me it seemed almost audible. When the question came, I knew it was the Lord.

Do you know Romans 3:23?

My first thought was, *Thank God, it's one I know.* I grew up in Baptist churches. Baptists lead people to the Lord down the Roman Road. Romans 3:23 is the first step.

So I whirled toward the Voice and quoted rather glibly at first, "For all have sinned, and come short of...Ah!...." I gasped as I saw it! The last four words fell feebly from my lips trailing almost to a whisper. "...the glory of God...."

The Voice spoke the revelation I'd glimpsed.

That's what happened in the fall. I crowned man with glory. Man sinned and fell short of the glory.

I felt I would faint with the revelation of the fall from such glorious heights to such heinous depths.

Then the Voice literally revived me with words based on Hebrews 2:10:

But the Captain of your salvation is bringing many sons to Glory.

I saw it for the first time! The circle of glory!

Man was crowned with glory. He fell from the glory. Through Jesus Christ he can return to the glory.

Then in a flash of revelation across my spirit I saw the predicament of the fall.

To the right, high and lifted up, was the place of the throne of God.

To the left, low and very low, stood Satan with man cringing at his side.

Between the two places there was a great gulf fixed.

I heard these words.

You always look at the fall from man's viewpoint. I want you to look at it from My point of view.

Within my spirit an automatic response arose, "I will be happy to, if You are pleased to show it to me."

The reaction of a natural man to a fallen son is to grab him and clasp him to his bosom. Had I clasped Adam to My bosom, I would have consumed him. My glory would have burned him up. And in him mankind. Satan would have stopped My words from coming to pass. For I had spoken that man would have dominion over the works of My hands.

Then I saw my first son, Terry. He stood tall, broad shouldered and thin at the waist with a large silver buckle fastening the leather belt around his blue jeans. I felt an urge to throw my arms around his middle in a tight squeeze.

What if you could not hug your son? For if you hugged him you would consume him.

I'm a hugging mother. So the Holy Spirit taught me with a hugging-mother parable. Back then when I hugged Terry he would sometimes say, "Aw, Mom." But he liked it and so did I. I couldn't imagine not being able to hug him. In fact I quickly considered how I probably would forget and he would be destroyed. I somehow felt a little of God's position at the fall of man.

And in a new way I understood how sin cannot stand in the Presence of God. It is written, "For our God is a consuming fire" (Hebrews 12:29). What does He consume? Sin.

I understood the precautions of the Old Testament.

God's glory stood behind a thick curtain in the Holy of Holies. The High Priest alone could enter there once a year on The Day of Atonement. And then he took great precautions.

It wasn't that God did not want mankind in His Presence. It was that man could not endure the glory of God.

I thought of when David brought up the Ark of the Presence on a cart rather than in the way God had instructed them to carry it for their own safety. When the oxen stumbled, Uzzah reached out to steady the ark, and died. It wasn't that God was just waiting to get him. God's glory broke forth to judge sin when the two came into contact. (2 Samuel 6; 1 Chronicles 13.)

Again I saw the scene with Satan clasping the cowering man and laughing up at God across the gulf. He thought he'd won. He thought he'd succeeded in separating God and his man forever. Satan knew that Adam, who once delighted in the Presence of God, would now be consumed by it.

His whining words ran together as he sneered over and over at God, "What-are-ya-gonna-do-now? What-are-ya-gonna-do-now? What-are-ya-gonna-do-now?"

I was made to know that God did not answer him.

But I also knew that God had a plan. A plan which began in heaven before the foundation of the world. God did not need to do anything now. He already had done something.

The Mystery of the Church

The New Testament calls God's plans "mysteries."

The Companion Bible says: The English word "mystery" is a transliteration of the Greek word *musterion*, which means a sacred *secret*...something *concealed* that can be revealed.[1]

Some of the mysteries the New Testament speaks about are: the mystery of Israel (Romans 11:25,26); the mystery of iniquity (2 Thessalonians 2:7); and the mystery of the church (numerous references).

God concealed His plan for the church throughout the Old Testament. Prophets prophesied about it, while they wondered of what and of whom they were speaking. Even the Gospel writers did not grasp the meaning of the mystery. It was not until a man named Paul came along that God revealed what He had concealed, the mystery of the church.

The Holy Spirit through Paul refers to it as: "...the mystery, which was kept secret since the world began" (Romans 16:25); "...the mystery, which from the beginning of the world hath been hid in God..." (Ephesians 3:9).

What a hiding place! It seemed to me there was a door in the midst of God marked "Top Secret."

When I saw the following passage I saw where the mystery led:

1 CORINTHIANS 2:6,7

6 Howbeit we speak wisdom among them that are perfect: yet not the wisdom of this world, nor of the princes of this world, that come to nought:

7 But we speak the wisdom of God in a mystery, *even* the hidden *wisdom*, which **God ordained before the world unto our glory.**

When did He ordain the plan?

Before the world!

For what purpose?

Unto our glory! Hallelujah!

Consider how strong this verse is in *The Amplified Bible.*[2]

1 CORINTHIANS 2:7 AMP

7 But rather what we are setting forth is a wisdom of God once hidden [from the human understanding] and now revealed to us by God; [that wisdom] which God devised and decreed before the ages for our glorification [that is, to lift us into the glory of His presence].

To lift us into the glory of His Presence! Hallelujah!

Now let's go on with the passage from the *King James Version.* We'll pick it up again at verse seven.

1 CORINTHIANS 2:7,8

7 But we speak the wisdom of God in a mystery, even the hidden wisdom, which God ordained before the world unto our glory:

8 Which none of the princes of this world knew: for had they known it, they would not have crucified **the Lord of glory.**

The Father of Glory (Ephesians 1:17), sent the Lord of Glory to lift up the man who had been crowned with the Glory, but had fallen from the Glory, back into the Glory of His Presence.

Do you see why I came to call the Bible "The Story of the Glory"?

If Satan had seen the plan, he never would have lifted God's spotless Lamb to the altar of the Cross where His innocent Blood could be shed to cleanse man to once again stand in the Glory of God's Presence.

The crux of the mystery is stated succinctly in Colossians 1:27:

COLOSSIANS 1:26,27

26 Even the mystery which hath been hid from ages and generations, but now is made manifest to his saints:

27 To whom God would make known what is the riches of the glory of this mystery among the Gentiles; which is Christ in you, **the hope of glory:**

Imagine Satan's dismay when the first man was born again!

When he saw that the Anointed One came to take up abode inside the man, and to become his hope of glory, I can picture the devil replacing his "What-are-ya-gonna-do-now?" chant with a cry of, "Curses! Foiled again!" and falling backwards.

Since Jesus arose, when a person believes in his heart that Jesus died on the Cross and that God raised Him from the dead, and confesses with His mouth the Lord Jesus, he is saved. He is born from above. He is born again.

At our new birth, the process of glorification begins and progresses according to the plan as we look into God's Word for His glory and yield ourselves to the Holy Spirit.

2 CORINTHIANS 3:18

18 But we all, with open face beholding as in a glass the glory of the Lord, are changed into the same image from glory to glory, *even* as by the Spirit of the Lord.

Again, *The Amplified Bible* makes it so clear:

2 CORINTHIANS 3:18 AMP

18 And all of us, as with unveiled face, [because we] continued to behold [in the Word of God] as in a mirror the glory of the Lord, are constantly being transfigured into His *very own* image in ever increasing splendor and from one degree of glory to another...

In the last hours before He appears to receive the church, it will change in ever increasing splendor and from one degree of glory to another, until there is only one more capstone of glory to be added to the Temple. That will be the glorious rapture of the glorious church (Ephesians 5:27).

Glory! That is what you and I are saved "to".

Salvation is not just what we are saved "from"—the devil and sin.

Salvation is what we are saved "to"—God and His Glory!

The church is destined to stand before God's face forever, in the Presence of His Glory (Ephesians 1:4; 3:21).

It is the last of the last days. God's glory is to be manifested in greater degree in His church. Very soon now we will walk the streets with our faces shining, and men and women will come to us to accept the Lord Jesus Christ they see within us.

The Blood of Jesus has everything to do with it. For it is His Blood that cleanses us, and covers us, and enables us to stand in His glory.

---

[1] *The Companion Bible* (Kregal Publications, Grand Rapids, MI 49501) Ap. 193, 211.
[2] *The Amplified Bible* (The Lockman Foundation, La Habra, CA, 1958, 1987).

Divine Circles 7

I nsight into the Blood and the Glory increases when one sees how they travel a circular route.

The Lord had shown me this path of His glory and man before I "accidentally" found the writings of A. E. Mitchell who articulated God's circles so well.

On a visit to Angelus Temple in 1982 I stumbled upon his set of ten small pocket books copyrighted in 1928 and entitled *The Philosophy of The Cross*.[1]

Mitchell was a minister, missionary, writer, and artist who departed earth for heaven in 1964 at the age of 87. Andrew and his wife, Jennie, founded the global missionary organization Go Ye Fellowship.[2]

Billy Graham wrote for the cover of Mrs. Mitchell's biography entitled *Jennie*, "The story of this remarkable woman should be read by every man, woman, and child, Christian and non-Christian alike. She truly adhered to Jesus' command to 'Go ye into every part of all the world and preach the Gospel to every creature.'"[3]

Richard Halverson, Chaplain, U.S. Senate, endorsing the same book said of the Mitchells, "No two people in my fifty-two years pilgrimage with Christ have so demonstrated authentic holiness as Jennie and Andrew."

Bible Doctrine's Circular Path

A. E. Mitchell said, "All Bible doctrine is built and runs its course in circular form."[4]

He gave the example of Jesus' illustration of His own mission.

JOHN 16:28

28 I came forth from the Father, and am come into the world: again, I leave the world, and go to the Father.

Can you see the circle?

Mitchell wrote, "All divine circles culminate in 'glory,' God being glorified...The gospel Godward is the great reason for the gospel usward. Much as Christ did for men on the cross, He did infinitely more for God. And this, we believe, is the best part of circle teaching. As the footsteps of Christ come usward, they bring salvation. As they return to God they bring to the Father utter and eternal pleasure and glory...The gospel usward is that which we are saved *from*, the gospel Godward is that which we are saved *to*...we are redeemed *to God*, and *to His glory*."[5]

Romans 11:36 shows the circle, "For of him, and through him, and to him, are all things: to whom *be* glory for ever. Amen."

The following passage reveals how God's Word travels a circular route.

ISAIAH 55:8-11

8   For my thoughts *are* not your thoughts, neither *are* your ways my ways, saith the LORD.

9   For *as* the heavens are higher than the earth, so are my ways higher than your ways, and my thoughts than your thoughts.

10 For as the rain cometh down, and the snow from heaven, and returneth not thither, but (except it) watereth the earth, and maketh it bring forth and bud, that it may give seed to the sower, and bread to the eater:

11 So shall my word be that goeth forth out of my mouth: it shall not return unto me void, but it shall accomplish that which I please, and it shall prosper *in the thing* whereto I sent it.

Rain and snow, in the natural realm, demonstrate the path God's Word travels. They come down earthward. They return heavenward in the natural process of evaporation. Yet they do not return without first bringing forth fruit upon the earth.

Likewise God's Word originates in Him, travels earthward, accomplishes, and then returns to bring God glory.

The Glory travels that path.

The Church travels that path.

The Blood traveled that path.

---

[1] A. E. Mitchell, *The Philosophy of The Cross*, (Go Ye Fellowship, P.O.Box 40039, Pasadena, CA 91114-7039).

[2] Go Ye Fellowship, P.O. Box 40039, 1550 E. Elizabeth St., Pasadena, CA 91114-7039.

[3] Robert Bryant Mitchell, Marietta Mitchell Smith, with Howard Hugh Wade, *Jennie*, (Isaiah Sixty: One Publishing Co., Weaverville, CA 96093).

[4] A. E. Mitchell, *The Philosophy of The Cross, As Interpreted in The Blood Line*, Vol. 4 (Go Ye Fellowship, Inc., P.O. Box 40039, 1550 E. Elizabeth St., Pasadena, CA 91114-7039) 14.

[5] Ibid., 14,15.

The Circle of the Blood 8

A. E. Mitchell wrote, "The Blood Line is a Circuit.... None of the 'precious' things of the divine economy are homed on earth, but in Heaven. The Blood has but One Terminal, that is in Heaven from whence it came."[1]

Before the Foundation of the World

The circular path of the Blood began in Heaven "before the foundation of the world" (1 Peter 1:18-20).

The Blood of Jesus was not an afterthought of the Creator taken in surprise at the fall of man. God never plays catch-up to Satan. If He did, Satan could lead God.

No. Before God created man He knew he would fall. Before God formed man He foreordained his redemption with "precious Blood."

Divine plans originate in the Father. Somewhere—in the divine council rooms of Heaven, perhaps—the Father must have put forth His plan for man.

Man would be spirit. In God's image. On God's order and kind.

Therefore, man would be able to fellowship God.

Man would be able to love God.

Man would be created to work with God—to have dominion over the works of God's hands. For such high eternal purpose man could not be a robot.

Spirit man would be given a soul—a mind, a will, and emotions.

Fallen Lucifer would tempt man's will.

Man would fall into the tempter's hand.

But God would redeem man.

God would design man for redemption in his creation. God would make man a creature of blood.

(God was not restricted to create creatures of blood. Angels were not created with blood. Lucifer was not created with blood.)

God would call man *Adam*, connecting him in the wonderfully revealing Hebrew language to blood (*dam*) and to the ground (*adamah*). Both blood and ground are red (*adom*).

God would put spirit man and his soul into a body of flesh made of the dust of the ground. (See 1 Thessalonians 5:23.)

The life of the flesh would be in the blood. (Leviticus 17:11,14.)

Man's body—an earthen vessel—could be broken and the blood poured out, a life for a life.

If a Divine One would go to earth Incarnate and live without sin in "a body prepared," His vessel could be broken and His perfect Life poured out in His Blood for the remission of all sin.

In some eternal moment, in some heavenly place, the One we call Savior agreed to fulfill the Father's great plan of redemption. First in Heaven, and eventually at Calvary, our Lord Jesus offered Himself through the Eternal Spirit, without spot to God. (Hebrews 9:14.)

The Psalmist records Jesus' words, in glorious contrast to the rebellious words of Lucifer, "Then said I, Lo, I come: in the volume of the book it is written of me, I delight to do thy will, O my God..." (Psalm 40:7,8). (See also Hebrews 10:5-10.)

In what is a great mystery, God the Son became, "...the Lamb slain from the foundation of the world" (Revelation 13:8).

1 PETER 1:18-20

18 Forasmuch as ye know that ye were not **redeemed** with corruptible things, *as* silver and gold...

19 But **with the precious blood of Christ, as of a lamb** without blemish and without spot:

20 Who verily was **foreordained before the foundation of the world,** but was manifest in these last times for you.

The Circular Blood Line

The Blood line began in Heaven.

It circled earthward first in revelation through types and shadows. For God had to reveal to fallen man the place and the power of the Blood of the Lamb to redeem him.

God Himself shed the first blood in type when He made coats of animal skins to cover man. Blood would cover man until he was again fit for glory.

The blood of every animal on every legitimate altar of Old Testament times was to reveal the Lamb slain from the foundation of the world.

LEVITICUS 17:11

11 For the life of the flesh *is* in the blood: and I have given it to you upon the altar to make an atonement for your souls: for it is the blood *that* maketh an atonement for the soul.

The precious Blood was manifested in the earth when Jesus came.

John the Baptist looked upon Jesus and said, "Behold, the Lamb of God, which taketh away the sin of the world" (John 1:29).

The earthly part of the Blood's path was consummated when the manifested Lamb poured out His life in His Blood on Calvary's altar.

The circle of the Blood turned upward again on the third day. Our Lord Jesus Christ arose—triumphant over death, hell, and the grave—and carried His own precious Blood into the Heavenly Holy of Holies where it was accepted for man.

The resurrected Lamb closed the circle giving glory to God the Father.

The powerful, redemptive Blood is returned to its Heavenly Terminal. There before the throne of the Living God, the Blood ever speaks "mercy" for man. (Hebrews 12:24.)

Oh! What a Planner! Oh! What a Plan!

[1]A. E.Mitchell, *The Philosophy of The Cross, As Interpreted in The Blood Line*, Vol. 4; 13,15. (Go Ye Fellowship, P.O. Box 40039, 1550 E. Elizabeth St., Pasadena, CA 91114-7039).

The Blood Line

9

God drew a Blood line—from Heaven to earth and back to Heaven.

Our question is: Can believers draw a Blood line?

In my quest after the place of the Blood of the Lamb as a primary weapon against the strategies of the enemy, I came across an amazing incident.

A minister and his wife, named Stevens, were conducting meetings in Canada in a large church. They had left their children at home in the southeastern part of the United States in the care of grandparents.

The Canadian meetings were inflicting great damage to the kingdom of darkness. Many were coming to new life in Jesus, and many were being set free from bondages of Satan.

Don Gossett gave the following account in his book *Praise Avenue:*

> Because of this success, the devil became infuriated and began to torment Brother Stevens with the thought that he was going to kill the Stevens' children.
>
> Brother Stevens said, "Devil, you're a liar! You cannot kill my children."
>
> To this, the devil seemed to say, "Oh, yes, I can, for I have put rabies upon the foxes in the woods adjoining your property."
>
> Immediately, Brother Stevens remembered the reports of friends who had seen foxes roaming on his land before he'd left Tennessee.
>
> In simple childlike faith, Brother Stevens gathered together three other believers. Together they agreed in prayer, and by faith they drew a blood line of protection around the Stevens' property...

A week later, Brother Stevens received a letter from his brother back in
Tennessee.

He said, "Today I was out walking. I walked around the edge of your
property. Lying on the boundary of your land I found five dead foxes. We
had the heads examined and found they were all rabid."

The foxes had dropped dead when they tried to cross the Blood line![1]

When Reverend Gossett heard this, he had his answer. For a long time
thieves had been regularly breaking into his ministry office vandalizing and
causing great devastation. The Gossetts installed security devices. They
worked with police. Nothing stopped the intruders. Until...

"When I heard this story," Don Gossett wrote, "I decided to draw a
Blood line...I called my wife and family together. By faith, we drew a Blood
line around our offices. That was in 1969. We've never had a break-in at our
offices since."[2]

Is there a Bible basis for drawing a Blood line?

Decidedly yes!

The Scarlet Thread

The Blood line runs like a scarlet thread from Genesis to Revelation
revealing God's great plan of redemption.

To work His plan, God chose a man, Abraham.

The man became a family.

The family became a nation.

Through this nation, chosen and separated, God would bring forth His
written Word, and eventually, "the body prepared" for the Lamb.

At the birth of the nation from a multitude of slaves, God met the
children of Israel in Egypt with the Blood line. In fact, He instructed them
to draw it themselves. For He particularly revealed the power in the Blood to
protect in the first Passover.

The Night Death Passed Over

After nine terrible plagues Pharaoh still refused to let God's people go.

With the tenth—a great terror—God would bring His people Israel out of the land of Egypt. (Jeremiah 32:21.)

Moses informed Pharaoh, "Thus saith the LORD, About midnight will I go out into the midst of Egypt: And all the firstborn in the land of Egypt shall die, from the firstborn of Pharaoh that sitteth upon his throne, even unto the firstborn of the maidservant that is behind the mill: and all the firstborn of beasts" (Exodus 11:4,5).

A close inspection of God's account is required to see what He revealed:

EXODUS 12:1,3,5-7,11-13

1 And the LORD spake unto Moses and Aaron in the land of Egypt, saying...

3 Speak ye unto all the congregation of Israel, saying, In the tenth *day* of this month they shall take to them every man a lamb, according to the house of *their* fathers, **a lamb for an house...**

5 Your lamb shall be without blemish, a male of the first year: ye shall take *it* out from the sheep, or from the goats:

6 And ye shall keep it up until the fourteenth day of the same month: and the whole assembly of the congregation of Israel shall kill it in the evening.

7 And **they shall take of the blood, and strike it on the two side posts and on the upper doorpost of the houses,** wherein they shall eat it...

11 And thus shall ye eat it; *with* your loins girded, your shoes on your feet, and your staff in your hand; and ye shall eat it in haste: **it is the LORD'S passover.**

12 For I will pass through the land of Egypt this night, and will smite all the firstborn in the land of Egypt, both man and beast; and against all the gods (princes) of Egypt **I will execute judgment: I** *am* the LORD.

> 13 And **the blood shall be to you for a token** upon the houses where
> ye *are:* and **when I see the blood, I will pass over you,** and the plague
> shall not be upon you to destroy *you*, when I smite the land of Egypt.

It is important to see that this plague was judgment.

Sin was judged in the day man fell. Man was due judgment. But God in mercy had held off the fullness of judgment.

On this night God would lift His withholding hand and allow the destroyer to execute the sentence of the law of sin and death.

A dilemma existed. The children of Israel, as the sons of Adam, were also due the stroke of judgment. And Satan knew it.

But God already had provided for the salvation of man. A Lamb was slain from the foundation of the world. The token of the Blood displayed upon their houses would withhold judgment.

Moses instructed the people how to draw a Blood line the destroyer could not cross.

EXODUS 12:21-23

21 Then Moses called for all the elders of Israel, and said unto them, Draw out and take you a lamb according to your families, and kill the passover.

22 And ye shall take a bunch of hyssop, and dip *it* in the blood that is in the basin, and strike the lintel and the two side posts with the blood that is in the basin; and none of you shall go out at the door of his house until the morning.

23 For the LORD will pass through to smite the Egyptians; and when he seeth the blood upon the lintel, and on the two side posts, the LORD will pass over the door, and will not suffer **the destroyer** to come in unto your houses to smite *you.*

Think about it.

The destroyer would rather have killed God's chosen ones. But he could not kill even one of their animals. A line drawn across their thresholds stopped him.

Was it a power inherent in the blood of the little lambs which held him at bay?

No!

When the head of the household applied the blood to the doorposts of his home, he entered the circle of the Blood from the point of time in which he lived. The Blood line he drew across the entryway to his home and loved ones represented the power in the Blood of the Lamb slain from the foundation of the world.

When God the Judge of all saw the blood applied in faith, He could look at that household through the precious redeeming Blood foreordained before the foundation of the world and judgment could legally be stayed.

Passover: A Continual Memorial

God instructed Israel they were to keep Passover a memorial, by an ordinance forever.

Since that night in Egypt the Jews have kept the feast of Passover.

I once spent Passover with a religious family on what the world calls "the West Bank." The Bible calls the particular place where I was "the mountains of Israel," or "Samaria." Because it is considered by many to be dangerous territory, my host family's relatives would not come to their home. So I was the only guest at the special Seder Meal.

The smallest child asked the question, "How is this night different from all other nights?" (See Exodus 12:26).

In answer, the English-speaking father throughout the long night's observance related the account of the Exodus to the children as if it had been their very own family which was delivered from Egypt.

I watched with interest when the middle of the three pieces of unleavened bread was hidden in the household and the children went to search for it. There was great joy when the bread was brought forth from its hiding place.

How precious is the blessing over the bread: Blessed art Thou, Oh, Lord, King of the Universe Who brings forth bread from the earth.

Of course, I thought of Jesus.

As a Jewish boy He kept the law. Every year of his life He kept Passover. He kept Passover those years He was training His disciples. But when He came to the last Passover He would keep, the Bible emphasizes His intense desire to eat it with them.

The *King James Version* translates His words like this, "With desire I have desired to eat this passover with you before I suffer" (Luke 22:15).

The Amplified Bible translates it, "I have earnestly and intensely desired...."

Knox translates it, "I have longed and longed...."

You see, the time had come when He could reveal that He was the bread without leaven (sin) which would be broken for man and come forth from the earth.

He could reveal that He was the Lamb whose Blood was shed for man.

LUKE 22:15,19,20

15 With desire I have desired to eat this passover with you before I suffer...

19 And he took bread, and gave thanks, and brake it, and gave unto them, saying, This is my body which is given for you: this do in remembrance of me.

20 Likewise also the cup after supper, saying, This cup is the new testament in my blood, which is shed for you.

Believers living under the New Covenant have the right to enter the communion of the Blood "which is shed for you" and to draw a Blood line Satan cannot cross.

If we do not have that right, we do not have a better covenant based on better promises. But we do! (Hebrews 8:6.)

In Egypt at the first Passover, they applied the blood with a hyssop branch. Since the Lord's Passion, we apply the Blood by faith. Because we believe in the power of the Blood in our hearts, we apply the Blood with our mouths over the doorposts of our lives.

Honor the Blood

The Holy Spirit brought to my attention a wonderful tract I highly recommend. Still in print today, it was written by W. B. Young, a leader at Keswick, who qualifies as one of our old-timers. It is entitled *Honor the Blood*.[3]

Reverend Young began with how Satan tries to break down the spiritual and physical life of the saint of God. He stated:

> There is no saint, weak or strong, who goes unnoticed by the Destroyer.

"Soulish ingenuity" Reverend Young emphasized is no match for satanic strategy. "The strongest efforts of resistance will crumble under the force of hell's fury when met by any other way than God's way."

Then through an excellent teaching Reverend Young expounded upon God's way.

> There must be a personal application of the blood of Christ in order to stem the tide of spiritual destruction in the life of the child of God.
>
> It was said of Moses that, "Through faith he kept the passover, and the sprinkling of [the] blood, lest he that destroyed the firstborn should touch them" (Hebrews 11:28).

It is a personal matter.

"The blood shall be to you for a token" (Exodus 12:13).

"When I see the blood, I will pass over you" (Exodus 12:13).

The blood, applied by sprinkling, was all that was required for peace of mind and rest of heart. It took away all fear of the destroying angel. It was not mere interest in the blood, nor belief in its power, nor appreciation of its worth that availed. It was the applied blood that counted. Truth was translated into action.

So it is with the blood of the Lord Jesus. It is effective against satanic floods when applied by faith. A proper application of His blood to a given situation, if the believer is operating from a cleansed position, always brings deliverance. It never fails...

As God built a hedge around Job, which limited Satan, so today He will do the same for any child of God who applies the blood to a given situation. The blood is the hedge that stops the Destroyer.

We will come back to this tract in a later chapter when we consider just how to apply the Blood of Jesus to the "given situations" in life today. But first we must consider in some detail another account from the Bible.

---

[1] Don Gossett, *Praise Avenue*, Box 2, Blaine, WA 98230.

[2] Ibid.

[3] W. B. Young, *Honor the Blood*, Osterhus Publishing House, 4500 W. Broadway, Minneapolis, MN 55422.

If Rahab Could...
We Can!

10

G od gave an amazing revelation of the power in the Blood to protect in the account of Rahab the harlot.

I sit this evening writing this chapter in Israel—not far south of Jericho. Out my window I see the mountains of Moab changing colors in the light of the setting sun. They lie east of the Jordan River in present-day Jordan. But from my vantage point, too far away to reveal detail, they appear as they must have 3300 or so years ago when the children of Israel passed through on their way to the Promised Land.

In these surroundings my mind wonders anew at the remarkable faith of a Canaanite harlot. For what Rahab did, the Bible says, she did by faith. (Hebrews 11:31.) And my mind wanders back easily to the circumstances of her world.

This whole country was filled with fear. The massive multitude of the children of Israel (perhaps 2 1/2 million) had destroyed the kingdoms that tried to stop their move toward the Land of Canaan.

The Bible describes the state of the area's kings; "Their heart melted, neither was there spirit in them any more, because of the children of Israel" (Joshua 5:1).

The inhabitants of Jericho, a Canaanite city-state, were terrified. Yet in the midst of a frightened population, one woman exercised faith so great it gained for her a good report from God and a place in two Bible halls of fame: the lineage of Jesus, and the elders of faith. (Matthew 1:5; Hebrews 11:2,31.)

Every circumstance of Rahab's life and society was against her exercising such faith.

The headlines—so to speak—of the day warned of impending doom.

Her religion was against her. The Canaanite religion sacrificed children in the fire and centered on sex. (Deuteronomy 13:10,11.) *The Revell Bible Dictionary* says about it:

> The religion of the Canaanites focused on fertility...Religious rites employed sex...to stimulate the gods and goddesses to grant fertility to the land and to their livestock...
>
> The moral and religious depravity of the Canaanites, portrayed in Scripture and revealed even more clearly in the materials recovered from Ugarit...(by archaeologists)...explains why God commanded Israel to totally destroy these people within the borders of the Promised Land. The war of extermination was a long-delayed divine judgment on the Canaanites (Gen. 15:16).[1]

Jehovah's plan seemed to be against Rahab. The Creator of the Universe determined it was time to execute judgment upon her society. And she lived in the most dangerous spot on the globe. Her house was on the city wall which God decreed must fall.

Follow Her Faith

Rahab's faith deserves close consideration. For it reveals a way to use the power of the Blood in the face of today's events.

Joshua sent two spies into Jericho. They lodged at the harlot's house, possibly because it would not arouse suspicion. When the king of Jericho heard it, he sent men after them. Rahab hid the spies under stalks of flax upon her flat roof while she managed to get rid of the king's men.

Before the Hebrew spies left she said to them:

JOSHUA 2:9-11

9 ...I know that the LORD hath given you the land, and that your terror is fallen upon us, and that all the inhabitants of the land faint because of you.

10 For we have heard how the LORD dried up the water of the Red sea for you, when ye came out of Egypt; and what ye did unto the two kings of the Amorites, that *were* on the other side Jordan...whom ye utterly destroyed.

11 And as soon as we had heard *these things*, our hearts did melt, neither did there remain any more courage in any man, because of you: for the LORD your God, he is God in heaven above, and in the earth beneath.

Rahab heard the same news everyone in town heard—the supernatural acts of Israel's God. Fear filled the hearts of the overwhelming majority. Faith filled Rahab's heart, for she decided to believe Jehovah must be the true God. Based upon her belief, her faith spoke.

JOSHUA 2:12,13

12 Now therefore, I pray you, swear unto me by the LORD, since I have shewed you kindness, that ye will also shew kindness unto my father's house, and give me a true token:

13 And *that* ye will save alive my father, and my mother, and my brethren, and my sisters, and all that they have, and deliver our lives from death.

Rahab dared to ask for the lives of her father, her mother, her brothers, her sisters—*and she wanted all their possessions*. Their material goods. Their belongings.

It's a good thing she hadn't talked to some people today. They'd have talked her out of such audacity.

It evidently pleased God. (Hebrews 11:6,31.)

Rahab also wanted a true token—a sign.

If the spies had not been running for their lives, they might have slain a lamb and placed the same token upon Rahab's doorposts which was sprinkled upon the Hebrews' doorposts when judgment was coming to Egypt forty years earlier.

This time a scarlet cord would have to do for Rahab and her family. A scarlet line would represent the Blood of the Lamb slain from the foundation of the world.

JOSHUA 2:18,19,21

18 Behold, *when* we come into the land, thou shalt bind this line of scarlet thread in the window which thou didst let us down by: and thou shalt bring thy father, and thy mother, and thy brethren, and all thy father's household, home unto thee.

19 And it shall be, *that* whosoever shall go out of the doors of thy house into the street, his blood *shall be* upon his head, and we *will be* guiltless: and whosoever shall be with thee in the house, his blood *shall be* on our head, if any hand be upon him...

21 And she said, According unto your words, so *be* it. And she sent them away, and they departed: and she bound the scarlet line in the window.

Sometime later, with no natural weapons, Israel executed God's plan to the utter destruction of Jericho.

For six days Jericho's trembling residents watched a strange processional. The Ark of the Presence, priests blowing trumpets of rams' horns, and the host of Israel compassed their city walls once each day. Yet no Hebrew made a sound with his voice.

On the seventh day Israel compassed the city seven times. At the seventh time, Joshua said unto the people, "Shout; for the LORD hath given you the city" (Joshua 6:16).

JOSHUA 6:20-23,25

20 ...and the people shouted with a great shout, that the wall fell down flat, so that the people went up into the city, every man straight before him...

21 And they utterly destroyed all that was in the city...

22 But Joshua had said unto the two men that had spied out the country, Go into the harlot's house, and bring out thence the woman, and all that she hath, as ye sware unto her.

23 And the young men that were spies went in, and brought out Rahab, and her father, and her mother, and her brethren, and all that she had; and they brought out all her kindred (Heb. families)...

25 And Joshua saved Rahab the harlot alive, and her father's household, and all that she had....

When the Word of God is *repetitive* it is for purpose. We are supposed to get the point.

Over and over the Bible emphasizes the saving of Rahab's loved ones.

The word translated *kindred* in verse 23 is the Hebrew word for families, plural. It indicates that extended families somehow related to Rahab were saved.

Mrs. Jeanne Wilkerson of Tulsa was held in high esteem as a teacher of the Word and a woman of prayer. She said that the Lord once spoke to her in prayer to this effect:

"Tell the people not to be concerned over My soon appearing because of lost loved ones. Tell them to name them to Me in prayer. Those whose names they call to Me in faith, I will see that they make it if I have to wrestle them on their beds in the nighttime."

Over and over the Bible emphasizes the saving of their material goods.

When I leave my home, as I must do in ministry, often for weeks at a time, I never fail to say, "Thank You, Lord, for the Blood of Jesus Christ. In the Name of Jesus I draw a Blood line around my property and possessions."

When I return all has been kept safe from thieves or storms.

I have learned to place my hands upon my luggage and to say, "In the Name of Jesus I apply the Blood of Jesus upon you. Pass over to (whatever destination) when I pass over."

When I do that the luggage always arrives on time.

Twice, in traveling hundreds of thousands of miles, luggage has been lost or stolen. Each time, I have seen a mental picture of the hurry I was in when I left and I failed to speak the Blood's hedge of protection around my goods. It is as though the thief is watching for an entrance. I have to remember to keep my watch with my mouth to keep him out.

If a Canaanite harlot's faith can protect family and goods, how much more can a New Testament believer's faith in the power in the Blood of the risen Redeemer protect loved ones and possessions.

If we cannot draw a Blood line around our loved ones and property in this hour of peril and even judgment, then we do not have a better covenant based on better promises.

But we can! (Hebrews 8:6.)

Tokens Displayed

The Bible calls the blood upon the doorposts of the Israelites that first Passover in Egypt "a token." (Exodus 12:13.) It calls Rahab's scarlet cord "a true token." (Joshua 2:12.)

Tokens are signs. They are to be displayed.

God gave the rainbow as His "token" that the world would never again be destroyed by water. (Genesis 9:11-17.) He has displayed that token somewhere upon the earth many times a day from that day to this.

We are to continually display the token of the Blood of Jesus and its power over the doorposts and boundaries of our lives. How? By faith. By the words of our mouths because we believe it in our hearts.

That's what the old-timers did when they would "plead the Blood!"

---

[1]*The Revell Bible Dictionary*, (Fleming H. Revell Company, Old Tappan, NJ), 189, 190.

Tokens:
Answer to Terrorism

11

Whurhen Jesus told us what would occur before His Second Coming, He said, "And there shall be signs...upon the earth distress of nations, with perplexity...Men's hearts failing them for fear, and for looking after those things which are coming on the earth..." (Luke 21:25,26).

A word that strikes fear to the hearts of men these days is *terrorism*. Though it takes various forms and comes from divergent groups, its real source is Satan. He is the Master Terrorist.

How interesting it is that the Bible describes his end as "...thou shalt be terrors, and never shalt thou be any more" (Ezekiel 28:19).

I have observed terrorist acts from a close view point—primarily, in Israel where I spend so much time.

On a recent trip, we took our seminar study group of 50 to Beit Lid, just about 5 miles from the Hebrew Language Center where I study Hebrew, and where we begin all our tours.

Beit Lid, a small covered bus stop, was typical of many throughout the land. In this tiny country—Israel is the size of New Jersey—the military bases are not far from home for the young men and women who make up the majority of Israel's forces. So they usually go home when they have time off, especially for Sabbath. Uniformed young Israelis waiting for buses as they are coming or going home is a familiar sight. Terrorists, sometimes car bombers, sometimes knife-wielding assailants, attack such bus stops with regularity.

Two months before we stood at Beit Lid, two suicide bombers had struck and killed more than 20 young soldiers, mostly girls. A Pentecostal pastor who lives in Israel and serves in the police, described to our group the horrors of cleaning up the scene.

Just a few days later on our study tour, we got off our bus to take pictures at a scenic point high above the Jordan rift. A young couple from California wanted their picture with me. We were walking into the overview area provided for scenic photography, when the husband said, "What's that?" I looked down to see about two feet from us a small military-green rectangular metal box. Two small black wires were attached to it.

Our regular bus driver, Moshe (Moses), is a Commander in the Israeli army. (All men serve until they are 55.) He determined it to be a land mine, probably stolen from the military by terrorists and placed strategically to do damage to innocent people who would take pictures there on the upcoming holiday. Moshe stationed two Israeli soldiers who were hiking the rift to watch the apparatus while we drove to the military base close by to report it.

We always make it a point to go to what the world calls "the West Bank." The Bible calls it "Judea and Samaria" and particularly tells the Jews to settle there when God brings them home in the last days before the Messiah comes.

One place I love to go in Judea is Hebron. It is the place where God cut "the covenant between the pieces" with Abraham for the land. (Genesis 15.)

It is also the place where the giants said "Boo" and the doubting spies shrunk to the size of grasshoppers in their own sight. (Numbers 14:22,28,33.)

Today the political giants of the world want Israel to give up Hebron.

Machpelah—the tomb of Abraham and Sarah, Isaac and Rebekah, Jacob and Leah—is in Hebron.

Jews and Muslims pray there under heavy military guard. But tourists have not been allowed there for a long time.

On our recent trip, I said to our guide, one of the first six Israeli families to settle in Hebron after the six-day war, "I hate it that we cannot go to Hebron."

He said, "Who said you can't go?"

We both knew who said it, but somehow what God said sprang up within our hearts. We checked with the people on the study tour—what a group!—and they wanted to go.

We hurried to the bus from the back side of Massada where we were walking down the Roman ramp when we had this conversation. Then we drove the back way to Hebron. Our eyes were blessed along the way to see herds of camels (actually dromedaries) with Spring babies alongside their mothers.

Our Jewish guide said to me, "Pray like you've never prayed before."

When we arrived, our guide got off the bus and spoke to the soldier in command. He came back to me.

"You'll have to swear that you are a descendant of Abraham and that you came here to pray."

"No problem," I said. I remembered Galatians 3:29.

I swore the same to the Israeli Commander and threw in a little Hebrew to convince him.

He said, "Well, maybe you. But not that bus load of Americans."

I said, "Yes, each one of them can swear the same."

And they did.

So with armed soldiers surrounding us, we walked up the hill to the huge edifice built over the caves in the time of Herod. They guided us to the cupola over Abraham and Sarah's grave and commanded, "Pray!" Our guide and the soldiers stood outside the door.

I went behind the small pulpit where rabbis usually stand and said, "I believe God has brought us here to pray. No tourists have been here in a year and we are here. I do not know what He wants us to pray, so we will pray in the Spirit."

That wonderful group lifted their voices in united prayer for ten to fifteen minutes.

When we left the cave area, a military jeep went ahead of our bus and one went behind to provide us escort out of Hebron and toward Jerusalem. The jeeps were equipped with strong search lights which constantly probed the sides of the road for it was now dark.

When we got through a dangerous junction where ambushes often occur, our guide was overjoyed.

About fifteen minutes after we crossed the junction we met bus number 60 from Jerusalem carrying Jewish commuters home to their settlement, Kiriyat Arba. (Joshua 14:15.) When bus 60 reached the junction, terrorists fired upon them from the sides of the road where they had waited in ambush. They hit the bus driver. Two young Jewish men were killed. But the bus just came to a stop. Some said it was a miracle that more were not killed. Perhaps it was an answer to prayer.

The next morning on our bus we prayed together again for the wounded and the families of the victims. And then we sensed an unusual anointing to pray the terrorists would be caught. Just a few days later the news reported the Israeli army apprehended those same three terrorists heavily armed and apparently on their way to a bombing attack.

A few days later suicide bombers hit a bus in the Gaza area. A young American Jewish woman, a student, was killed, along with seven others. Her father came from New York to accompany her body back to America. They were on my El Al return flight. I watched the entourage which met them at JFK to honor them.

Somehow I am familiar with such things. In Israel. But not in Oklahoma City.

Exactly one month to the day after our experience in Hebron the tragic bombing of the Murrah Federal Building occurred. Terrorists, "home-grown" the media called them, unbelievably struck at the heartland of America.

There is a terrorist—Satan—who is striking with great wrath because he knows his time is short. The Bible specifically tells us how to overcome him—with the Blood of the Lamb, by the word of our testimony, and by committed lives.

I was so proud of the brave Oklahomans and the witness of their faith broadcast to the world from the buckle of the Bible belt. What the devil meant for evil definitely cost his kingdom.

A Blinking Sign

One day, years ago, the Lord made this Scripture come alive to me.

PHILIPPIANS 1:28

28 And in nothing terrified by your adversaries: which is to them an evident token of perdition, but to you of salvation, and that of God.

The Bible instructs us not to be terrified by our adversaries. It further specifies "in nothing," in no thing.

Just by doing this we send them "an evident token." Remember "token" means sign. An evident sign is one easily seen. Just not being terrified by our adversaries sends them an easily read sign.

A sign of what?

Of their "perdition."

Perdition means doom.

The day the Lord revealed this to my spirit I saw it like this.

When we are not terrified, it's like we put up a huge blinking neon sign in the face of Satan and his demons.

"You're doomed! You're doomed!" the message flashes.

And that's not all it says. The Bible says it is to them "an evident token of perdition, but to you of salvation...."

It also blinks, "I'm saved! I'm saved! I'm redeemed! I'm redeemed!"

Satan and demons are not all-knowing. They don't know your heart. They can only read your countenance. And they are observing you. The original Hebrew of the following verse shows us that.

PSALM 27:11

11 Teach me thy way, O LORD, and lead me in a plain path, because of mine enemies.

This is one of my favorite Psalms. So I read it often. When I got a new Bible recently it had a reference to the last phrase that my previous Bible did not have. It gives the original Hebrew of "mine enemies," as, *those which observe me.*

I ran a reference and found this in the original Hebrew of other Scriptures.

What kind of signs are you sending those who observe you?

If you are not afraid, they won't stay around to read, "You're doomed! You're doomed!"

When you get up in the morning, send the right signals.

Don't say, "Oh, I'm so depressed." Those who observe you will laugh with glee and stay around to feed your mind with fear and sadness.

Say, "Praise the Lord! Oh, I'm so glad for this new day! Thank You, Father, for Your great plan of redemption! Thank You, for the blood of Jesus! I place the token of the Blood between me and mine and all the power of the enemy."

Those who observe you will flee as if in terror!

Going About Safely In These Last Days

We never take a group to Israel unless we know it is the will of God and that we have the timing of God.

"There is no safer place than the center of God's will," I wrote to my parents some years ago to assure them after terrorists trained in Libya attempted to enter Israel from the sea near the school where I study.

About that same time a crazed man had killed several people in a post office in Edmond, Oklahoma. You would have thought the safest place in the world was the post office in Edmond. But, no, the safest place is the center of God's will.

Every morning when we start our day on the tour bus, we read aloud together Psalm 91. Every verse is alive with meaning to us. And we trust its provision implicitly.

Then we quote Revelation 12:11. And we place ourselves under the protective power of the Blood of the Lamb. Usually, we sing the chorus of the old song, *Under the Blood*.

Years ago, a great man of God, so like Jesus, Brother Philip Halverson, said to my husband in an airport when Kent was feeling the pressures of travel, "Isn't it good to go about in the service of the Lord."

That's how I see my life. And the lives of all committed Christians. We simply go about in the service of the Lord.

How wonderful it is that we can go about under the Blood.

But we must display that token with our mouths.

You can walk around the place where you work or go to school and say, "In the Name of Jesus I draw a blood line around this place Satan cannot cross."

I believe no terrorist can cross a Blood line drawn in faith.

Put up the right signs. Put up the token of the Blood. Put up the sign of faith.

Jesus is Coming Soon!

Let's close our chapter by going back to where we began it. When Jesus gave the signs preceding His coming he instructed us, "And when these things begin to come to pass, then look up, and lift up your heads; for your redemption draweth nigh" (Luke 21:28).

Hallelujah!

Jesus is coming soon!

Satan is headed to the pit!

And until that day, we will overcome him with the Blood of the Lamb, the word of our testimonies, and the commitment of our lives to God.

Thank God, for illumination into the power in the Blood of Jesus and how to access that power in our everyday lives by pleading the Blood.

Defining: To Plead

12

Pleading the Blood has nothing to do with begging.

Pleading the Blood has nothing to do with mechanical repetition of empty words.

Plead in the Scriptures is legal terminology.

Before we consider the "why" and "how" of pleading the Blood, we will define our terms to agree with the Bible's use of *plead, plead my cause,* etc.

Reev

One Hebrew word translated *plead* is the root word *reev.* In its verb form it means: *to strive, contend, to conduct a legal case....* In its noun form it means: *dispute, controversy, case at law.*[1]

It is variously translated as the emphasized words in the Scriptures below:

> 1 SAMUEL 24:15
> 15 The LORD therefore be judge, and judge between me and thee, and see, and **plead my cause**, and deliver me out of thine hand.

> 1 SAMUEL 25:39
> 39 And when David heard that Nabal was dead, he said, Blessed be the LORD, that hath **pleaded the cause** of my reproach from the hand of Nabal, and hath kept his servant from evil....

(How interesting this wording is..."hath pleaded the cause...and hath kept...from evil...." Just what we can do in pleading our only case, the Blood of Jesus!)

JOB 13:6

6 Hear now my reasoning, and hearken to **the pleadings of my lips.**

(The book of Job is filled with the imagery of the courtroom. The need of a mediator, an arbitrator, between God and Job is the theme. We have used only one verse from Job.)

PSALM 35:1

1 **Plead my cause**, O LORD, with them that **strive** with me....

PSALM 43:1

1 Judge me, O God, and **plead my cause** against an ungodly nation: O deliver me from the deceitful and unjust man.

PSALM 74:22

22 Arise, O God, **plead thine own cause**: remember how the foolish man reproacheth thee daily.

PSALM 119: 154

154 **Plead my cause,** and deliver me....

PROVERBS 22:22,23

22 Rob not the poor...neither oppress the afflicted...

23 For the LORD will **plead their cause,** and spoil the soul of those that spoiled them.

PROVERBS 23:11

11 For their redeemer is mighty; he shall **plead their cause** with thee.

ISAIAH 1:17,18

17 Learn to do well; seek judgment, relieve the oppressed, judge the fatherless, **plead** for the widow.

18 Come now, and let us reason together, saith the LORD: though your sins be as scarlet, they shall be as white as snow; though they be red like crimson, they shall be as wool.

ISAIAH 3:13

13 The LORD standeth up **to plead**, and standeth to judge the people.

ISAIAH 50:6-8

6 I gave my back to the smiters, and my cheeks to them that plucked off the hair: I hid not my face from shame and spitting.

7 For the Lord God will help me; therefore shall I not be confounded: therefore have I set my face like a flint, and I know that I shall not be ashamed.

8 He is near that justifieth me; who will **contend with me?** let us stand together: who is mine adversary? let him come near to me.

(Here it is! This is prophetic of Jesus and His triumphant death and subsequent justification. He says, "Who will **conduct a legal case or suit** with Me?" The answer, of course, is that no case or adversary can stand against Him. Therefore, our case, the Blood of His Cross, is sure.)

JEREMIAH 50:34

34 Their Redeemer is strong; the LORD of hosts is his name: he shall throughly **plead their cause**, that he may give rest to the land, and disquiet the inhabitants of Babylon.

LAMENTATIONS 3:58

58 O Lord, thou hast **pleaded the causes** of my soul; thou hast redeemed my life.

MICAH 7:8,9

8 Rejoice not against me, O mine enemy: when I fall, I shall arise; when I sit in darkness, the LORD shall be a light unto me.

9 I will bear the indignation of the LORD, because I have sinned against him, until he **plead my cause,** and execute judgment for me: he will bring me forth to the light and I shall behold his righteousness.

Shawfat

The marvelous Scripture below uses the Hebrew word *shawfat* with the Lexicon giving the meaning in this verse as: *plead; have controversy together.*[2]

ISAIAH 43:25,26

25 I, even I, am he that blotteth out thy transgressions for mine own sake, and will not remember thy sins.

26 Put me in remembrance: let us **plead** together: declare thou, that thou mayest be justified.

Now we know what the Bible means by *plead.*

Let us proceed to learning how to plead our case by pleading the Blood.

---

[1]Francis Brown, *A Hebrew and English Lexicon of the Old Testament,* Based on the Lexicon of William Gesenius (Oxford University Press, Oxford, London, New York), 936, 937.
[2]Ibid. 1047, 1048.

Pleading Our Case: Redeemed by the Blood!

13

A great courtroom procedure has ensued since the fall of man.

God the Father is God the Judge of all. (Hebrews 12:23.)

Jesus Christ, the Righteous, is our Advocate. (1 John 2:1,2.) *The American Heritage Dictionary* defines *advocate* as: One that argues for a cause. One that *pleads* in another's behalf; an intercessor.[1]

Satan is the Prosecuting Attorney—the accuser.

REVELATION 12:10,11

10...for **the accuser of our brethren** is cast down, which accused them before our God day and night.

11 And they overcame him by the blood of the Lamb, and by the word of their testimony; and they loved not their lives unto the death.

The title "the accuser of our brethren" reveals Satan's character and, therefore, his ongoing activity. (That's why I try not to listen to accusations against brethren. I know where they originate. And I fear to be found on the accuser's side in any matter.)

The Bible is the Book of the Law.

Someone has said, "If man's redemption is to be real, it must be solidly lawful."

Redemption is the crux of the matter.

Adam exercised his free will and fell into the hand of the enemy.

The Blood of the Lamb redeemed man *from* Satan's hold and *unto* God and His plan.

The American Heritage Dictionary gives this definition of *redeem*: "To recover ownership of by paying a specified sum."[2]

As a child, I heard an evangelist tell a story which helped me understand redemption.

A father and his small son worked together and built a toy boat. They whittled out its hull, painted it red, and attached a white sail. Then they enjoyed many happy hours sailing it in the river running through their village.

Somehow the father died. When the boy sailed the boat alone, it brought back good memories. Until... One day a big wind caught the little sail and carried the boat down the river faster than the boy could run after it. Out it sailed into the sea.

The boy missed his boat so much for the long time it was gone.

About Thanksgiving time, he was overjoyed to see his little boat appear in the toy shop window.

He ran inside and said, "That's my little boat in the window! My father and I made it and it was lost to the sea."

The shop owner said, "The little boat was brought in by fishermen who found it. I'll let you have it for what it cost me."

The boy had no money. But he went to work. He cut wood. He sold papers. He did everything he could think of to do. Each day he counted his money. And each day he held his breath as he passed the toy shop to see if the little boat was still there.

At last, on Christmas Eve, he had enough money. But had someone bought the little boat for a gift? How thankful he was to see it still in the window.

When he came out of the shop, he clasped the little boat to his chest and cried, "Little boat! Little boat! You're twice mine! I made you! And I bought you!"

God made us and He redeemed us. He redeemed us not with silver and gold, but with "precious Blood."

Far-reaching Redemption

Not only are we delivered out of the hand of Satan, the Bible pointedly states our redemption is threefold.

GALATIANS 3:13,14

13 Christ hath redeemed us from the curse of the law, being made a curse for us: for it is written, Cursed is every one that hangeth on a tree:

14 That the blessing of Abraham might come on the Gentiles through Jesus Christ; that we might receive the promise of the Spirit through faith.

We are redeemed:

    1) From the curse of the law.

    2) To the blessing.....

    3) That we might receive the promise of the Spirit.....

The attacks of "the accuser of the brethren" are always in one of these three areas. He strives to rob us of our redemptive rights by attempting to: 1) Bring the curse of the broken law upon us—poverty, sickness, death. 2) Keep our inheritance from us. 3) Prevent us from living in the fullness of the power of the Holy Spirit within.

All this is legally ours.

At the new birth believers are translated out of the kingdom of darkness and into the kingdom of light. We have redemption now through His Blood! (Colossians 1:13,14.)

We are citizens of Heaven—now! (Philippians 3:20.)

We may live by the laws of the Spirit of life in Christ Jesus which have set us free from the laws of sin and death. (Romans 8:2.)

But Satan will not just roll over and let it happen for us.

We are commanded to give him no place. (Ephesians 4:27.) He and his accusations are to be overcome with the Blood of the Lamb to which he has no defense.

Grace Roos, who lived a supernatural, overcoming life and even picked out the day she left earth for Heaven without sickness or disease, wrote: "Satan has no answer to the Blood of Jesus. He has no weapon to withstand its devastating effect upon him. He is absolutely vulnerable to its overcoming power. Knowing this, he hides what is happening to him and seeks to deceive us into settling for less than we wanted. Legally Satan was defeated at Calvary, so legally we are his victors through Christ who gave us power of attorney in Luke 10:19. However, he is not yet imprisoned and so cunningly works his devilish craft to ever deceive and hide his limitations...."[3]

"Say So"

PSALM 107:2

2 Let the redeemed of the LORD say so, whom he hath redeemed from the hand of the enemy.

Pleading the Blood with our mouths lines up with this Scripture. The Bible instructs us to **say** that we are redeemed.

If the enemy tries to put the curse upon you, say that you are redeemed from the curse of the law.

Say, for example: "I am redeemed from the curse of the law. You can't put that (name it) on me. According to Deuteronomy 28:61 all sickness is the curse of the law. But according to Galatians 3:13 I am redeemed from the curse of the law and I say so. I am redeemed by the Blood of the Lamb. I overcome you, Satan, by the Blood of the Lamb and by the word of my testimony."

Let the redeemed of the Lord say so! That is pleading the Blood!

Witness

In the courtroom scene, we have a witness. First John 5:8 declares that the Blood is a witness.

Again, Mrs. Nuzum wrote in an old tract someone sent me:

> A witness is expected to speak, and Hebrews 12:24 tells us that the blood does speak...A witness, or his testimony, is always taken to the place of trial. Colossians 1:12 tells us that God "hath made us meet to be partakers of the inheritance" in Christ. If Satan disputes this and seeks to keep us out of any part of this great inheritance, we are to ask that the witness, the blood of Jesus, be allowed to speak, and the blood will declare that Jesus bought it for us on the cross and that it is all ours.
>
> The next verse says that God "hath delivered us from the power of darkness." If Satan tries to use his power over our spirit, soul, or body, we must call for the witness and the blood will again speak to God for us and declare that Jesus, on the cross, fully delivered us from all the power of the enemy, so that he now has no power to put sin, sickness, pain, or disease upon us...
>
> If Satan tries to put some of the curse upon us or keep us from getting rid of some of the curse we had upon us, we are to call for the witness. The blood of Jesus will again testify that Christ set us free from all the curse when He was made a curse for us...
>
> It is the blood of the new covenant, the pledge that we are to have all that is promised in it. If Satan tries to keep us out of a promise of God,

we are to call for the witness and the blood will testify that Jesus bought the things promised and His precious blood was the price paid...

By faith, steadfastly hold the witnessing blood just where you want God to work and let the precious blood of His dear Son speak, testify, cry unto God for us. God worked mightily when the blood of Abel cried unto Him—how much more powerfully He will work when it is the blood of His well-beloved Son that cries.

Stanley H. Frodsham, biographer of Smith Wigglesworth and longtime editor of *The Pentecostal Evangel* wrote in an editorial, "It is written, 'They overcame by the blood of the Lamb.' They overcame hell's dragon with the simple weapon of Heaven's Lamb. When the dragon seeks to overcome you, take him to Calvary where through that sacred blood his power was brought to naught. Magnify that blood and the Lamb who shed the blood. Give bold testimony to the power of that blood." [4]

Bold Testimony

Speaking of bold testimony! John Osteen, Pastor of Lakewood Church in Houston, Texas, is boldness personified. I heard a minister say about him, "The devil says every morning when John Osteen arises, 'Oh, no! He's up again!'"

Brother Osteen's comments on Revelation 12:11 inspire boldness to all who read them in his book *Unraveling the Mystery of the Blood Covenant:*

The blood of Jesus says, "You have victory!"

After you become a covenant-person, Revelation 12:11 takes on new meaning. It tells you how you can overcome the devil. You overcome him by three things:

First, by the blood of the Lamb. When the devil comes against you, hold up your Bible and say to him, "Devil, I want you to see this. This is

God's everlasting Blood Covenant that Jesus cut for me. Christ's righteousness has been imparted to me. All God's power and blessings are mine. I command and charge you, Satan, look at that blood. You are already defeated."

Second, by the word of their testimony. You can boldly say, "Satan, I dare to stand on God's promises. It is written... They are tried and proven. I'm a covenant-person, and God will not break His Word with me."

Third, they loved not their lives unto the death. These Christians made an unqualified commitment to God. All God had was theirs, and all that they had was His. They were covenant-men, covenant-women. They were willing to even sacrifice their own lives, if necessary, to live for Jesus and tell others about His way of living.

You don't overcome Satan by your tenacity. You don't overcome him by your good works. You don't overcome him by your goodness. You don't overcome him by your own holiness or righteousness. You don't overcome him by your mental agility. You overcome him by the blood of Jesus Christ.

Just present that blood to Satan and say, "See the blood, devil. The One who shed this blood crushed your head and took your power. He's my Lord!"

Yes, the blood of Jesus Christ speaks to you today. It cries out—

You are justified.

You are redeemed.

You have peace.

You are God's property.

You have eternal salvation.

You are clean.

You are washed.

And you have victory.

Oh, the wisdom of God, and the greatness of His wisdom! How unsearchable are His ways! How mighty is His wisdom for the human race and His love for man![5]

Our Only Plea

In the early '70s my husband, Kent, worked for eighteen months in Pennsylvania. During the summer of 1971 I took a leave from my job and the children and I spent three months with him in Beaver, Pennsylvania.

We liked antiques and we had lots of fun traveling the back roads of Pennsylvania and Ohio looking for goodies.

Following a crudely painted sign advertising something for sale we came upon an old Ohio farmhouse and a fascinating family who lived there. Not long out of the hippie culture they were newly born again and glowing with the light of new birth.

When they discovered I worked for a ministerial association, the wife, still dressing rather like a "hippie-chick" begged us to come back again and again to teach them the Bible.

One day she shared a dream she'd just had.

In her dream she stood third in a long line of people waiting before a beautiful gate to enter Heaven.

Father Abraham met each one and asked their qualifications for entry.

The first man in line said, "I was a Boy Scout leader. I devoted all my free time to young boys preparing them to be good citizens."

"That's good," came the reply. "But is there anything else?"

Other good deeds were mentioned along the same line.

"That's good. But is there anything more?"

"No."

With a wave of the authority figure's hand, the applicant was denied entry.

The second person was a woman. In response to the request for her qualifications she said, "I was a Sunday School teacher for thirty years."

"That's wonderful. But is there something else?"

She offered nothing else.

"Entry denied."

My friend thought in her dream, *Oh, they've done wonderful things and they're not getting in. I've never been anything but a hippie!* And she felt great concern.

"Next," came the call.

It was her turn!

"And what are your qualifications to enter Heaven?"

She was surprised at her quick answer, "I plead the Blood of Jesus Christ!"

"Open wide the gates!" Father Abraham cried with a sweeping movement of his arms indicating her abundant entrance into glory.

There can be no argument against pleading the Blood. It is our only plea!

---

[1]*American Heritage Electronic Dictionary*, Houghton Mifflin Company.

[2]Ibid.

[3]Grace Ryerson Roos, *Spiritual Warfare*, "Meditations for Today," Box 3612, Bartlesville, OK 74006.

[4]*The Pentecostal Evangel*; Assemblies of God Archives, Springfield, MO.

[5]John Osteen, *Unraveling the Mystery of the Blood Covenant*, John Osteen, Box 23117, Houston, TX 77228. 61, 62.

How To...   14

E arly on in my quest, a strong desire arose within me to know the truth
    the old-timers in Pentecost understood about the Blood of Jesus.

The months, even years, of research into their teachings and experience
brought wonderful rewards. Later we'll see what happened spiritually at the
turn of the century to produce such successful "sprinklers" of the Blood. But
in this chapter and the next I have selected a few examples of just "how" they
did it.

I must say as a pre-requisite to these selections that I noticed the
following attributes common to all of them:

1) They had strong faith in the Blood.

2) They believed they had the right to use the power in the Blood by faith.

3) They recognized they needed to operate from a cleansed position.

Some Scriptures they had faith in for their use of the Blood, in addition
to others we've already discussed, are:

ROMANS 3:24,25

24 Being justified freely by his grace through the redemption that is in
Christ Jesus:

25 Whom God hath set forth (foreordained) to be a propitiation through
faith in his blood....

HEBREWS 11:28

28 Through faith he kept the passover, and the sprinkling of blood, lest
he that destroyed the firstborn should touch them.

1 PETER 1:2

2 Elect according to the foreknowledge of God the Father, through sanctification of the Spirit, unto obedience and sprinkling of the blood of Jesus Christ....

A Witness From Keswick

W. B. Young says, "The Holy Spirit, Who is the Infallible Teacher, will make real to each one, His way of working this 'mystery' of the wonder-working power of the blood of Christ to meet every thrust of Satan."[1]

Then in commenting on Revelation 12:11, he gives some "how-to" guidelines:

> In this verse He has given three general guidelines. 1. The basis of our power and authority over all the enemy: "the blood of the Lamb." 2. The word of our testimony. This is the practical application of our belief in "the blood of the Lamb." When the conflict is close and fierce with the Adversary, our testimony will be directed to him. Jesus practiced this truth. Under the protection of the blood of Christ and with the authority vested by Christ himself, unafraid and unflinchingly notify Satan that he is a defeated foe, that he has no right or power in a given situation because you are moving against him and his activity with the precious blood of Christ. God promised His people that when He saw the blood He would deliver. God will keep His part of the covenant. Our responsibility is to "sprinkle the blood." It is God's part to deliver. 3. All aspects of the self-life must be reckoned "unto death" if Satan is to be defeated. The redeemed saint who is cleansed from sin must become a selfless saint in order to become a victorious warrior. When these three premises are met, then the child of God is able to exercise his heritage of spiritual authority. The unlimited power of the blood of the Lord Jesus will be loosed.

Some successful warriors that I know take this simple stand of faith, "I cover my home with the blood of Jesus to protect occupants and possessions from any influence, Satan, that you or your evil spirits would try to exert. I bring to bear the power of the blood of Jesus to bind you." It is also helpful to remind him that God said that what we "bind on earth" He would "bind in Heaven." The applied blood of Jesus always calls his bluff. He was stripped of his power at Calvary. He is utterly helpless against the blood of Christ...

Do not limit the power of the blood of Christ to what you understand. There is no greater mystery in the Christian life than the worth and power of His blood. Apply it by faith. Be a child of God who practices the "sprinkling of the blood of the Lord Jesus Christ." Sprinkle it anywhere there is evidence of pressure, tension, or any kind of satanic effort to thwart the complete will of God in your life. God wants it for a witness, "And to Jesus the mediator of the new covenant, and to the blood of sprinkling, that speaketh better things..." (Hebrews 12:24). Praise the Lord, the Blood speaks!

---

¹W. B.Young, *Honor the Blood*, Osterhus Publishing House, 4500 W. Broadway, Minneapolis, MN 55422.

Holding the Blood

15

A nother thing I noticed in the old-timers was perseverance. They would "hold" the Blood against the devil until victory came.

You will see this in these excerpts from Mrs. C. Nuzum's teaching entitled "Resisting the Devil."[1]

> Faith in the blood of Jesus, and in what God has said in His Word, when exercised in testimony against the devil, will always cause him to flee. First Peter 5:9 says, we are to be steadfast in resisting the devil. We are never once to think he *can* remain or keep evil upon us, because God has said that if we resist him he *will* flee, and God's Word *cannot* fail. So there is only one thing to see to, and that is to resist the devil until he goes, be the time long or short...
>
> Your own mouth can hasten the victory greatly. God says in Mark 11:23, you shall have what you say if you do not doubt. Say, "I refuse to have this sickness," no matter how much Satan tries to make you feel or see it...
>
> The Word tells us that the Blood overcomes Satan and that he *does* flee. Plant your feet upon these truths, use the remedy and never relax until victory comes. It must come because God has said it will...
>
> I arose one morning and found that I could not stand—I reeled like a drunkard. I said, "This is of you Satan; I *hold* the Blood against you, and declare on God's Word that it does now overcome you, and that you do *now* flee." The enemy was stubborn, but I continued to believe and

repeat what I said until every trace of the trouble was gone. I then did a full day's hard work, and have had no return of the evil....

A lady resisted smallpox for herself and family. One of them broke out with it, but she seated herself by the bed and told God she would not cease to resist until the disease went. Every bit of the disease disappeared, and no one else took it. She resisted steadfastly...and found Him faithful who had promised....

I have found that as I continually meet Satan with the Blood, and never release until he flees, the Blood works quickly and more powerfully. I am sure it will do the same for you, dear reader, if you will set to your seal that God is true, that the Blood is infallible, and His promises sure. Galatians 6:9 says, "Be not weary...for in due season we shall reap, if we faint not." God's time is now, and, if you are all right, you should have immediate victory; but you must begin with a fixed purpose never to stop until you have full victory. Jesus won it for you on the cross, and all you have to do is to hold fast without a doubt, or waver, or weakening until it is felt and seen. God the Almighty One says you shall reap if you do not faint—which means ceasing to believe and to resist, or becoming less earnest and persistent. The more stubborn Satan is, the more earnest and persistent you must be.

Rachel Teafatiller, a woman used by God in prevailing prayer for fifty years now, told me, "People quit too soon."

The old-timers I read after kept the Blood applied until they saw the victory they knew was theirs.

Grace Roos expresses it well from her own and others' experiences:

For all that is wrong in your life and circumstances begin to declare, "There is power in the Blood of Jesus to set everything right, Satan. I declare to you that HIS atoning Blood works now to minister defeat to every evil work of yours and to bring it down to nothing." DECLARE IT! The saints in Revelation "overcame him by the Blood of the Lamb and the Word of testimony." What worked for them works for us also. God's Word is ETERNAL TRUTH.

...Satan recognizes your advantage over him. He will seek to shake your stand but refuse to be shaken. He will try to shove you off the rock onto the quicksands of feelings, but REFUSE to be shoved. Stand FIRM and testify of your victory until you have it in your hand.

A prayer warrior was taking a strong stand against the enemy... Weary with the stubborn opposition she was meeting, she prayed, "Lord, what can I do?"

The voice of the Lord deep within replied, "You do not need to hold out against the enemy; HE HAS TO HOLD OUT AGAINST YOU!"

...SATAN is ALREADY DEFEATED AND HE MUST DEFEND HIS BLUFF of strength and victory over and over again; while we share in Christ's victory over him and we HAVE ALL THE ADVANTAGE! This is written from better than 20 years of experience... Tremendous victories have been realized as we refused to budge from our position of faith...

...About six or seven years ago my husband had a mole on his right temple that became badly infected. As weeks passed it grew progressively worse. Pains began to shoot down his chin and behind the right eye, burning and itching—a real cause for concern. Together we prayed and believed for its healing. Then **daily** by faith, we applied the Blood of Jesus to this tormented spot, ministering death to its continuance, binding its power to remain. We recognized it to be the work of Satan, part of the curse our Lord Jesus delivered us from and thus we claimed our exemption... Refusing to accept this curse daily as the months rolled by, the day came when my husband reached for the mole out of pure habit, and it was GONE. It had dropped off sometime during the day. All that remained was a tiny scar showing where it HAD BEEN.

My husband has often used this illustration: Two generals were discussing their respective armies. One said, "My men are the bravest soldiers in the world!" The other replied, "My men may not be the bravest soldiers, but they will stay in the battle fifteen minutes longer than any others!"

As Christians we may not be the bravest people, but God has so equipped us that by His grace and Spirit we can withstand the enemy—or outlast him in his stubborn stand.

One thing we MUST understand, whether we see it or not, the Blood of Jesus undermines Satan's structure of lies. Satan "covers up," he bluffs to the very last, hoping to get you to believe God's Word does not work for you!

God has told us to STAND and then WITHSTAND (Ephesians 6:10-14) and He has made clear in His Word just HOW to go about it. If we do not heed His instructions, preferring our own method of warfare He will permit us to reap the defeat that is waiting for us. There is NO SUBSTITUTE for God's battle strategy—mark it down! Our total victory is in the powerful virtues of the Blood of Jesus.[2]

Society's problems running rampant in the Twentieth Century are not more powerful than the Blood of Jesus.

Where one has God-given authority—in your own life; in the lives of your children; for pastors, in the lives of their flock; etc.—any stronghold of Satan can be destroyed by holding the Blood of Jesus upon it.

Christian parents are not powerless against demons of drugs. Preventative action can be taken with the training up of the child in the way he should go. Preventative action can be taken with the Word of God and the Blood of Jesus daily in your mouth speaking boundaries Satan cannot cross.

But if Satan has gained a stronghold through drugs—or whatever—into your child, you can "hold" the Blood of Jesus against him as you have learned to do here until he flees.

Your child doesn't even have to be with you. Meditate upon Scriptures concerning the Name of Jesus and the Blood of Jesus until they are real to you. Then when you sense you've got it, make your move. Rise up and say, "In the Name of Jesus I hold the Blood of Jesus against you demons of drugs—or whatever—that have lodged in my child's mind and body. Jesus defeated you and now in His Name I hold His Blood against you and you have to flee...."

Then keep the Blood applied. How? By faith. Remember faith is in two places, in your heart and in your mouth. (Mark 11:23; Romans 10:9,10.) Because you believe in your heart you say it with your mouth. And you keep saying it until the demons give up—which they must do!

This is not prayer. This is taking your God-given authority over Satan and his forces. This is overcoming the devil.

In January 1995, a beautiful young career woman from New York told me how she persevered in holding the Blood against a long-entrenched condition in her body. She had suffered with several ruptured discs in her spine for five years.

Her roommate told me the pain was terrible to watch. Her friend could not lift the coffee pot or open the heavy door to their apartment.

The young victim's medical history included four MRI's and the doctors' conclusion that she must have surgery. She was reluctant to do so because of the permanent effects it would have on her back.

Somehow she got our first set of teaching tapes on the Blood. She heard how the old-timers would "hold" the Blood on a problem. And she decided to "hold" the Blood on her discs. She reported to me, with her roommate standing beside her, that now she was completely free of pain and another MRI showed a perfect back.

The Blood Against Temptation

The old-timers knew resisting the devil also included resisting temptation to sin. And they resisted sin with the answer to the sin problem, the Blood of Jesus.

Mrs. C. Nuzum wrote:

> ...We are to resist his dominion over us by refusing to obey him, or let any of our members serve him. We are to resist the sins, appetites, passions, and evil desires which he has put upon us, by asking God to put the Blood of Jesus against the devil and the evil within, and then believe that God does put the Blood there when we ask Him to do so, and that it does what God says it will do—overcomes the devil and destroys his work. We are to overcome all fear, depression, unbelief, wavering and halfheartedness in the same way...believe, because God says it does, that the Blood of Jesus now overcomes them, and assert upon God's unfailing Word— "The Blood of Jesus overcomes the devil and all he has done." When you see anything in you that produces the transgression, remember that His Blood will take that away... No matter in what way the enemy comes, whether in discouragement, temptation, sickness, or any other way, he is overcome by the Blood of the Lamb and by the word of your testimony."[3]

Another young career woman from New York told me how when she read Mrs. Nuzum's book, it brought light to her about how to combat the temptations of the Twentieth Century.

Temptation is tailor-made. Demons don't usually tempt people to drink alcohol who never had a drinking problem. But they do tempt delivered former alcoholics.

The Bible indicates demons come back to the houses they left. Periodically demons return to see if they can get back inside. Such temptations are not sins. They can be easily overcome with the Blood of the Lamb and the word of one's testimony.

One can say, for instance, "Satan, that's you trying to get me to smoke one reefer. In the Name of Jesus I resist you with the Blood of the Lamb. You have to go. It is written, 'Resist the devil, and he will flee from you.'"

In every confrontation, you can overcome the enemy.

You'll have to have the same attributes the old-timers had, but you can do it.

---

[1]Mrs. C. Nuzum, *The Life of Faith*, (Gospel Publishing House, Springfield, MO 65802), 60-63.

[2]Grace Ryerson Roos, *Spiritual Warfare*, "Meditations for Today," (Allonim Associates, P. O. Box 3612, Bartlesville, OK 74006), 10-13.

[3]Mrs. C. Nuzum, *The Life of Faith*, 51,54,61,62.

Rewards for Overcoming 16

od's Word commands us to overcome evil. (Romans 12:21.)

God's Word commends those who overcome the wicked one, evil spirits, and the world system. (1 John 2:13,14; 4:4; 5:4,5.)

God's Word gives us authority, weapons, and tells us exactly how to overcome.

Then finally, God's Word promises eternal rewards for being overcomers!

Our Risen Lord's promises to the overcomer in the beginning chapters of Revelation are astounding! (Revelation 2:7,11,17,26; 3:5,12,21.)

And the Book closes with, "...I am Alpha and Omega, the beginning and the end...He that overcometh shall inherit all (these) things..." (Revelation 21:6,7). The glories of eternity future are the things under discussion.

Better Resurrection

I have come to see from the Word of God that there is rank in resurrection. The Bible speaks of "better resurrections." (Hebrews 11:35.) Some will have more glory, if you will. (1 Corinthians 15.) Some will rule over more than others. This is all determined, it seems, by faithful service during our earth lives.

We are saved by grace through faith, and not of works. (Ephesians 2:8,9.) But after we are born again we are to do the good works God ordained us to walk in here on earth. (Ephesians 2:10.)

At the judgment seat of Christ we will receive reward for the good things done while we (our spirits) lived in our bodies. (1 Corinthians 3:12-16; 2 Corinthians 5:10.)

At some point job assignments will be given for the ages to come!

Just before Peter departed earth for glory he urged the believers not to be "short-sighted." (2 Peter 1:9.) Short-sighted people see only this life. Peter advised them what to do to receive an "abundant entrance" into the glory world. (2 Peter 1:4-11.)

While it is good to prepare for earth's life; it is far greater to prepare for eternity.

Overcoming the enemy is a God-ordained good work. It brings peace and provision to life on earth. Far beyond that, however, our victories over Satan bring glory to God and obtain for us the eternal reward of the overcomer.

This earth life is a precious time. It is too valuable to waste. Somehow being here in this place of trial offers us the mysterious opportunity to be a recognized overcomer throughout eternity.

Oh! What a Planner! Oh! What a Plan!

The Young Can Do It!

My 14-year-old granddaughter, Kylie, has heard me preach about these things all her life. She's preparing for this life by getting a good education. But she's also preparing for the big picture—eternity future.

Considering that temptation is tailor-made and that there is reward for overcoming the enemy, Kylie said to me about a year ago, "Mi-Mi, I'm going to be an overcomer. I'm going to overcome the devil in what he tempts teenagers with most, rebelling against their parents. I'm not going to let him make a generation gap between me and my dad and mom."

Kylie does such a sweet job of it that I once asked her, "Kylie, are you ever even tempted? It seems to me you just get along with each other without any problems."

"Oh, yes, Mi-Mi," she answered, "the devil tempts me every day."

I asked her to tell me the mechanics of how she handles it.

She said, "Sometimes I have to go in my room and take my pillow and scream into it, 'In the Name of Jesus I plead the Blood of Jesus over me. Satan, I won't be in strife with my parents. I love my parents. I am close to my parents and we are friends. And, devil, you can't do anything to me to break that friendship.'"

She also shared with me how she uses the Blood of Jesus for protection, against peer-pressure temptation, and to approach God in prayer on the behalf of her friends.

Home: Heaven on Earth

Kylie's parents have aimed toward God's promise that our homes can be "as the days of heaven upon the earth." (Deuteronomy 11:18-21.)

Satan's strategic assault against our homes has undermined our nation and is a direct affront against the revealed will of God for family life.

God commands us to be overcomers. The first place we must overcome him is in our domains. We don't have authority over our neighbors. But we have authority at home.

Why not accept the challenge and launch a counter-attack against the enemy in your home? Don't just lie down and let the devil hold high-carnival at your address. Resist him! You know how to do it!

(Now there are situations where people one does not have authority over refuse to stop allowing the enemy access to themselves and to abuse others through them. Sometimes for peace and well-being one must physically change the circumstances of life and home.)

What we are addressing here, primarily, are the homes of Blood-washed believers who desire God's best but whose homes rival those of the world for turmoil.

Your home can know heaven's peace. God will receive glory when you overcome Satan's attacks. Your family will be blessed. Our nation can be blessed. And you and your family members who take an active part in triumph over the wicked one will receive the overcomer's reward for victory on a major front in today's fight of faith! (1 Timothy 6:12.)

Earthquakes   17

We have records to show how the power in the Blood of Jesus released by faith in the hearts and mouths of believers provided protection during earthquakes from the beginning of the Twentieth Century to what is now its end.

Carrie Judd Montgomery (1858-1946) is described by the *Dictionary of Pentecostal and Charismatic Movements* as: A minister-teacher, writer, editor, director of faith homes, and social worker whose ministry spanned more than sixty-five years....[1]

She and her businessman husband, George, established the Home of Peace in 1893 in a large three-story Victorian house near Oakland, California. From then until now the home has served as a Bible training school, a faith home, an orphanage, a church, and a missionary service agency.

It withstood many earthquakes to do so.

Wayne Warner, Archives Director for the Assemblies of God, told how it survived the terrible San Francisco earthquake of 1906:[2]

> Mrs. Montgomery would never forget the night of April 18, 1906, when she was awakened with a peculiar sense of imminent danger. She believed that God wanted her to by faith put the blood of Jesus over their house and Home of Peace nearby. Then she went back to sleep. "When I again awakened, the house was rocking violently and it seemed almost as though it were lifting from its foundations."[3]
>
> Across the bay San Francisco lay in ruins, and many buildings in Oakland were also damaged. The Home of Peace, which suffered no serious damage, became a refuge for people who had fled San Francisco.

Those same heavenly factors—the leading of the Holy Spirit, and the applying of the Blood of the Lamb by faith—worked together to protect an entire church family, their homes, businesses, and belongings, in the powerful earthquake that struck at 4:31 a.m. January 17, 1994.

Awakening Sound

The Los Angeles Times of January 18 reported: A deadly magnitude 6.6 earthquake—the strongest in modern Los Angeles history—ripped through the pre-dawn darkness Monday, awakening Southern California with a violent convulsion that flattened freeways, sandwiched buildings, ruptured pipelines and left emergency crews searching desperately for bodies trapped under rubble.

A California couple described to *The Times* how they were awakened, comparing it to the 6.5 quake, in 1971. "This one felt much worse. It was much harder, a hard jolt. The '71 one swayed...."

The Times continued their article, "This one did not sway. It slammed..."

Some time later experts discovered the unusual way earth's plates hit together along a previously undiscovered fault line. This resulted in widespread damage like that of an even larger magnitude quake. And it caused the sound to which Southern California awoke on that Monday morning.

Pastors Arland and Brenda Steen and members of Thousand Oaks Christian Fellowship awakened to the same loud sound.[4] But some of them also heard another sound. *A supernatural recording from their Sunday night service a few hours earlier.*

Here's the story.

The Spirit and the Blood Agree

Brenda Steen had been experiencing the direct leading of the Holy Spirit for several weeks. The saving factor for the Steens and their church was, she *yielded* to the Spirit's guidance, just as Carrie Judd Montgomery did.

To illustrate the importance of yielding to the Spirit's leadings, I will go back a little.

I shared how in early 1993 I began a search which the Lord answered with a revelation of the Blood of the Lamb. When I talked about some of these things privately with my friend, Gloria Copeland, she said, "You need to share this with the body of Christ." She insisted that I come to Fort Worth to do that. It was with a certain amount of fear and trembling that I did so in the Fall of '93.

Brenda Steen requested the tapes. She said the Lord impressed her to listen to them three times and then to transcribe them.

Then the Lord impressed her to preach the series exactly in the order they were preached at Eagle Mountain Church.

(Arland ministers at the Sunday morning services and Brenda on Sunday nights.)

Sunday night after Sunday night she preached.

The week before the last session she sat on the steps of the altar praying. A sense of caution stirred in her heart. "What is it, Lord?"

Make much of the Blood.

For days she'd heard that phrase in her spirit. But this day it was a warning.

Brenda began to pray a Spirit-led prayer, "Father, I plead the Blood of Jesus over this building...."

Then came the final Sunday night of the series.

The Holy Spirit's clear direction to the Steens was to close the series with communion.

Three months before at our final service in Fort Worth, Pastor George Pearsons of Eagle Mountain Church approached me just before the service.

I remember the look on his face and exactly how he approached me.

"Mrs. Brim," he said, very kindly, but with the air of authority vested in the office he fills, "it is perfectly all right if you do not want to do this, but I have prepared the elements for Communion. I believe I have heard from the Lord that He wants us to close this way."

I thought about the material I needed to cover and considered the time element. Then I had the witness in my spirit that this was indeed the will of the Lord.

On that Sunday night in Thousand Oaks the Lord led the Steens to close in exactly the same way.

Preceding Communion, Brenda spoke with an unusual anointing.

"How many want a revelation of the Blood tonight?" she began.

She preached on The Blood Line from before the foundation of the world. She emphasized the first Passover and how they took "a lamb for a house" and drew a blood line which stopped the destroyer. She brought in Rahab and the scarlet cord, emphasizing the saving of their possessions. She closed with Jesus' last Passover wherein He disclosed that He was the bread and His Blood was the Blood of the New Covenant which was shed for us.

The Holy Spirit surely filled her mouth for she spoke as the oracle of God when she declared quite loudly, "I don't care if we do live in Southern California. I don't care if my house is on top of a fault line. My house will not be destroyed!"

The pastors invited the people to receive Communion "a Lamb for a house."

Pastor Arland said, "Instead of taking it as a congregation, the head of each household led the Communion for their own family, praying a Blood line of protection over each family member and their property."

It was a holy time.

Testimonies of Deliverance

Brenda Steen sat straight up in bed at 4:31 a.m. only a few hours after dismissal of the Sunday night service. She heard the sound of the powerful quake first. But then she heard another sound. It was the sound of her own voice, *I don't care if we do live in Southern California. I don't care if my house is on top of a fault line; my house will not be destroyed!*

Person after person would testify to hearing the same supernatural recording as they gave testimony the following Wednesday night of the miraculous protection they all experienced.

One child said, "I wasn't afraid. I heard Pastor Brenda's voice."

As it turned out, the Steen's house was near the previously undiscovered fault line which erupted to cause widespread devastation. (Both LA and Ventura counties, including Thousand Oaks, were declared Federal disaster areas.) The houses on either side of the Steens lost china, mirrors, light fixtures, and suffered structural wall damage. Only one broken vase and a few cosmetic hairline cracks gave evidence that the Steen's house was shaken.

Pastor Arland went to the church as soon as possible. He especially wanted to check on their valuable collection of old Bibles and books. He knew they had not fastened the tops of the bookshelves to the wall. They merely rested on larger bases. How happy and amazed he was to see that the tops of the cabinets had merely danced to the edges of the bases and stopped. All was well with the church building.

And all was well with the true church, the people.

Kenneth Copeland Ministries televised the story. And an excellent account by Melanie Hemry, along with pictures of those giving individual testimonies, was published in the *Believer's Voice of Victory*, July 1994.[5]

I'm borrowing freely from Ms. Hemry's story and mixing it with some testimonies given to me in order to share the wondrous works of God with you.

"Nothing Was Broken"

Stuart Schlosser awoke to the shaking and rolling that could only mean one thing—earthquake!

"I heard the shouts of the children awaking. Jumping out of bed to get to them I began to hear loud crashing sounds like things breaking and exploding. My wife joined me as we made our way down the darkened hallway for the electricity had gone out. We got all the children under the doorways and began praying.

"We began by thanking Jesus that He was here with us, then as the rumbling sounds seemed to get louder we began pleading the Blood, first over our home, then ourselves and our neighborhood, then we mentioned wherever the center might be. At that point one of the kids said we needed to plead the Blood over my business so we did.

"Once the shaking stopped we had the children come into our bedroom and we prayed again and rested on our bed. I found a flashlight and went through the house to see what damages we had. When I went through the twins' room I noticed the dresser mirror was shattered all over the floor and that we all had walked across it while getting the girls out of their room. I quickly made my way back to our room to check everyone's feet and there wasn't one cut on our feet. Praise God!

"Once daylight came we began to assess the damages finding some broken glass but all else looked okay."

At 9:30 that morning, Stuart left home to try and make his way to his Subway Shop located in Northridge. He didn't know then that Northridge sat over the epicenter of the earthquake. He didn't know that a scant mile and a half from his business, one whole floor of the Northridge Meadows Apartments had collapsed killing sixteen people. He didn't know that the University of California at Northridge science building—across from his business—had burned and half the dormitories had been destroyed.

"There was a strange glow in the sky," Stuart recalls, "and parts of the expressway were missing. Police cars directed traffic off the freeway and onto surface streets.

"As I approached the shop I noticed many shattered windows in neighboring businesses. I wanted to just turn around and go home but I continued on. When I pulled into the shopping center where my Subway shop is located I noticed some of my neighbors had damages to their stores... I pulled up in front of my store and just sat there staring into the store. Wow! Not one broken window! I then continued into the store to find things had scooted around and things had fallen from the shelves, but besides a few ceiling tiles that had fallen things looked pretty good.

"I began to thank God for the Blood covering that had been prayed over my business and for children that reminded me to pray for the business during the quake.

"I talked to many Subways during the following few days and was amazed to hear of all the damages they had incurred, especially with broken windows and Neon lighting which my store has in excess. But not one tube of Neon had cracked.

"God spared my business. But that's not all. The week following we broke all sales records for this location. January is typically our slowest month. We continued to have very strong sales for quite some time afterwards."

"There Was No Fear"

Keith Wengler's shift at UPS began that morning at 4:30. Keith was standing next to the conveyor belt waiting for packages when the earthquake exploded underneath him.

Panic-stricken people ran in every direction. Some rushed for the door while others hid under the belt. The building shook with a deafening roar.

Outside, trucks clanked together. Keith had lived through earthquakes before, but without question this was the worst he'd ever experienced.

In spite of the turmoil around him, Keith could think of only one thing. *My family! What's happening at home?*

"Just as suddenly as that thought flashed through my mind," Keith says, "I remembered the Blood. I prayed for my family. There was no fear. None, whatsoever. I drove home in peace."

When he arrived, Keith found his house and family safe and secure. Although the earth beneath them had trembled and shaken violently, it had succeeded only in moving one picture and knocking over the teddy bear collection that belonged to Keith's wife, Leigha.

"Everything was perfectly intact," Leigha says. "We were protected by the Blood!"

Miracle in Mobile Home Park

"My husband was working and not at home when I woke up at 4:31 a.m.," recalls Jennifer Clark.

"Our house was shaking violently. I could feel the back end of the house being lifted off the jack stands. Our waterbed was thrown in the air. I screamed, 'In the Name of Jesus, I pray the Blood of Jesus over my children, myself, and my house!'"

Instantly, the house settled back in place.

"Then I heard our ten-year-old daughter, Christina, shout, 'I plead a Blood ring around this whole park!'

"The next morning I saw indentations in a perfect line marking where the trailer had lifted on one end and wrinkled the metal. I believe when I prayed an angel set my home back down."

Fifty to ninety percent of all homes in mobile home parks in the area were devastated. Yet, in Jennifer Clark's mobile home park, only three out of 240 were lost. Jennifer believes those three were damaged before Christina got the words 'I plead a Blood ring around this whole park' out of her mouth.

"More Powerful Than Any Earthquake"

Mrs. Juanita Pryor testifies: "I grew up in California. I was living in Los Angeles during the February 9, 1971, earthquake and received the Lord and was baptized on February 14, 1971—the Sunday immediately following it— and have been walking with the Lord ever since.

"Living in California, you become accustomed to the earth moving now and then, but you are ever conscious of the 'big one' that is promised. On January 17, 1994, I thought the 'big one' had finally come.

"Sunday evening, the night before the quake...Pastor Brenda Steen was preaching about the power in the Blood of Jesus. She talked about its power to protect us against all kinds of catastrophes, including earthquakes...

"At 4:31 the following morning, we were jolted awake by the strongest earthquake I have ever experienced...Unlike previous quakes, and there were many, this one moved us up and down as opposed to side to side.

"Then suddenly, from deep within me, a boldness rose and I began to shout at the top of my lungs, 'I plead the Blood of Jesus over this house. I plead the Blood of Jesus over us.' My husband and children joined. I felt as if we were speaking directly to the quake itself and forbidding it to do us or our property any harm...

"We gathered the family and sang songs about the Blood for a long time. Hours later, we surveyed the damage and found that nothing was broken. Pictures had fallen off the walls, crystal and ceramic lamps had fallen, glasses had fallen from shelves. Things were everywhere, but not a single item was cracked, broken, or even chipped.

"We heard numerous reports from neighbors of the damage that was done. Two doors down, it took $40,000 to fix everything. But we didn't have to spend a dime.

"Our home became a peaceful refuge for another family who needed a place to stay. When my friend walked in she said, 'I can relax now.'

"There is truly power in the Blood. We know firsthand that it is more powerful than any earthquake."

God Hath Remembered

Several thousand aftershocks, some of them as large as 5.5 magnitude, and violent crime, plagued the area for weeks after the first quake.

On January 26, nine days later, Larry and Suzi Fox experienced the power in the Blood for protection against gang-related crime.

The Fox house was quiet as Suzi turned out the lights and prepared for bed. She didn't expect Larry home from work until late. As the general manager of a restaurant—the only one in its chain that had remained open since the quake—he had been extremely busy in recent days.

At 11 p.m. Suzi made her usual bedtime check on Chelsea, their two-year-old. Walking into the bedroom, she was surprised to see Chelsea's wide eyes staring back at her.

How strange. Chelsea isn't usually awake at this time of night. Her spirit suddenly alert, Suzi, sensed the warning of the Holy Spirit. *Something's wrong. Larry is in trouble!*

"Chelsea," she said, "we need to pray for Daddy." Without hesitation, Suzi prayed the Blood of Jesus over Larry and called forth angels to protect him. Then she picked up her Bible and prayed Psalm 91, "Father, I thank You that Larry abides under the shadow of the Almighty...."

At 11:15 p.m., Larry was working quietly in his office at the restaurant, finishing up the day's accounts. The restaurant doors were locked, both safes closed and secured for the night.

Suddenly Larry's office door crashed to the floor as two gunmen stormed in upon him. "Get to the floor!" screamed one of them, holding a pistol to Larry's head.

"Let's kill 'em now!" shouted the other as he shoved two of Larry's co-workers into his office at gunpoint.

Larry lay on the floor with an astounding sense of peace. Praying in tongues under his breath, he listened to the gunmen with calm—until he heard them say something that sent chills down his spine.

"We'll put them in the freezer," one gunman said.

"Oh, God, not the freezer!" Larry knew their walk-in freezer was equipped with the internal mechanism allowing the door to be unlocked from inside. But that mechanism was broken in the earthquake.

"There were two safes visible," Larry explains. "Most of the money was in the upper safe, but they acted like they couldn't see that one. They told me to open the lower safe."

Larry crawled to the safe and opened it, trying to anticipate their next move. Shockingly enough, there was no "next move." The gunmen simply grabbed the money and left, leaving Larry and the cooks completely unharmed.

Six days after the robbery, Suzi Fox gave birth to their second child—a son. They named him Zachary, which means, *God hath remembered.*

"The Lord Made a Difference"

Certain things impressed free-lance writer Melanie Hemry when she covered the story. The rest of this chapter is the close of her article:[6]

Although each story of victory is precious, what is most striking about the experiences of those at Thousand Oaks Christian Fellowship is their consistency. These are not isolated incidents. The testimonies reported here could be repeated by every member of TOCF for *not one of them lost a life or lost a home in the earthquake or its aftermath.*

Perhaps even more importantly, they didn't lose the peace and security in their families. Unlike the thousands of California children who were so shaken...they required psychiatric help, many of the children from the Steen's church ended up more confident in God's protection than ever before.

After one strong aftershock, for instance, four-year-old Justin Riddle ran to his mother and said, 'Mommy, did you feel the earth shake?'

"Yes, I did," Donna Riddle answered. "Were you afraid?"

"Naw..." shrugged Justin, "I just pleaded the Blood."

Justin is too young to know his response to the earthquake is different from that of many other children. But it is...and Pastors Arland and Brenda Steen are thrilled about it.

Pastor Arland said, "When the time of calamity came to the land of Egypt during Moses' day, the Lord made a difference between the Egyptians and the Israelites. As time moves forward in these last days there'll be earthquakes, famines, wars and rumors of wars. But there will always be a difference between the world and the Church."

---

[1]Burgess/McGee, Editors, Alexander, Assoc. Ed., *Dictionary of Pentecostal and Charismatic Movements*, (Zondervan, Grand Rapids, MI 49530), 626, 627.

[2]Wayne Warner, *Home of Peace Celebrates Centennial*, (Assemblies of God *Heritage*, 1445 Boonville Ave., Springfield, MO 65802-1894) Fall 1993, Vol. 13, No. 3, 18,19.

[3]Carrie Judd Montgomery, *Under His Wings* (Oakland: Triumphs of Faith, 1936), 149.

[4]Thousands Oaks Christian Fellowship, P. O. Box 3875, Thousand Oaks, CA 91359. Phone: 805-499-7045.

[5]Melanie Hemry, *When the Earth Shakes*, (Kenneth Copeland Ministries, *Believers Voice of Victory*, Fort Worth, TX, 76192-0001), July 1994, Vol. 22 No. 7.) 6-9.

[6]Ibid.

Anticipated Questions

18

I want to touch on a few honest questions which may arise concerning these things.

Q: Why did some Christians suffer loss in the California earthquake while others were protected?

I certainly don't have all the answers to this question which could apply to the much broader spectrum of *life*. Yet there are two biblical requirements for cooperating with God to receive the blessing and protection He wants to give every believer—even every man—that will help us better understand...

1) We must be doers of His Word. (James 1:22.)

2) We must be followers of the Holy Spirit.

In being a *doer* of the Word and not a *hearer* only, for instance, one would not just know Revelation 12:11, but one would in faith apply the Blood of Jesus.

It was not enough in Egypt just to agree God had a good plan. They had to do God's plan. They had to apply the blood to the doorposts. God's Word is His revealed plan. It is not enough to mentally assent to that plan. We must do it.

There are many things the written Word of God does not reveal. It does not tell you whom you should marry, how to invest your money, whether or not there will be a storm or an earthquake tomorrow morning, etc. Here we must follow the Holy Spirit's leadings in our everyday lives. And here again, we must *hear* and *do*—we must *hear* and *obey*.

The Holy Spirit leads the children of God. (Romans 8:14.) He is our indwelling guide. (John 16:13-15.) He directs our paths. (Proverbs 3:5,6.) He is not slack in His job.

But men have to *listen* to Him. Men have to hear the voice of the Holy Spirit within their spirits. (Proverbs 19:20; 20:5,18,24,27.) Our own actions can cause us to be keen of hearing or dull of hearing. Sometimes people, even preachers, are too busy to hear the Lord. Often people allow the sounds of this world to drown out the still small voice of the Lord.

Men also have to *yield* to the Holy Spirit. Even when we do hear Him, we must yield to what we hear. One preacher said after a terrible accident which took his wife's life, "Something told me to wait thirty minutes longer before we started on our trip. But I just shrugged it off."

Most of us have shrugged off true leadings of God.

Q: How can you tell if it's God warning you or the devil trying to scare you?

If I can't tell immediately, and usually I can, I test the spirits. I say, "According to the Word of God I bind the devil's power to deceive me with the Blood of Jesus. I will not let Satan's forces operate. If that is You, Lord, speaking to me, please say on."

If it goes away, it was the devil.

The Lord wants us to test the spirits. If it is the Lord, He is faithful to speak again.

For example, I have traveled hundreds of thousands of miles by air. Every time I get on an airplane I touch the side as I enter the door and say to the plane, "In the Name of Jesus pass over to (and I name the destination) under the Blood of the Lamb without incident."

This is based on faith in the Scripture where Jesus said to the disciples entering the boat, "Let us pass over unto the other side" (Mark 4:35).

At that point I check my spirit. If something was wrong and there was some factor which would prevent my taking authority over the flight, the

Holy Spirit would warn me. (And I would be required to take heed.) In all these years, He has never done so. Therefore I have always boarded in peace.

A couple of times though the devil has tried to speak up and scare me. But when I put the leading to the test mentioned above, it went away, and the flight went well.

Since I learned to do this I cannot remember a frightening flight.

Q: What about the Name of Jesus?

There is no competition between the holy wonders of God's kingdom. There is no competition in the Godhead. There is no competition between the weapons (plural) of our warfare. (2 Corinthians 10:4.) There is no competition between the Name of Jesus and the Blood of Jesus.

Jesus said, "In my name shall they cast out devils..." (Mark 16:17).

The Bible also says, "And they overcame him by the blood of the Lamb, and by the word of their testimony; and they loved not their lives unto the death" (Revelation 12:11).

I have emphasized the Blood of Jesus because the Lord alerted me that the devil had almost stolen its primary place from us.

A good way to say it is, "In the Name of Jesus I plead, or apply, the Blood of Jesus."

The Word of God, the Name of Jesus, the Blood of the Lamb, and resources of Heaven are made available to us in our earth walk. We need to possess all the secrets revealed in the Word pertaining to the power availed us.

Then, too, in remembering the place of the Blood, the Word of God is a blood covenant. Every provision and promise therein are ratified by the Blood of Jesus Christ.

As David Ingles' marvelous song declares—some have called it the most scripturally revealing song on the Blood they've ever heard—everything we have in God is *On the Basis of the Blood*![1]

---

[1]David Ingles, *On the Basis of the Blood*, David Ingles Productions, P. O. Box 1924, Tulsa, OK 74104, 918-455-1595.

The Rains of the Spirit 19

The blood of Jesus redeems us *from* the hand of the enemy and the curse of the law. God wants us to know the power of this truth in the last days.

But there is a last day application of the Blood of Jesus God also wants us to know. It is of far greater glory. It involves what we are redeemed *to*. And its basic tenet is found in this redemption Scripture:

GALATIANS 3:13,14

13 Christ hath redeemed us from the curse of the law, being made a curse for us: for it is written, Cursed is every one that hangeth on a tree:

14 That the blessing of Abraham might come on the Gentiles through Jesus Christ; **that we might receive the promise of the Spirit through faith.**

Redeemed is a Blood word. I have come to see clearly that the most glorious part of our redemption by the Blood of the Lamb is *"that we might receive the promise of the Spirit."*

All that entails, individually and as the body of Christ, we will not address here. The end of this book is confined to a glimpse at the "Spirit of Glory" to be revealed in the last days and the role the Blood must play for its manifestation among us.

The Spirit of Glory

The Bible calls the Holy Spirit "the Spirit of Glory." (1 Peter 4:14.)

It tells us in Romans 8:11 that Jesus Christ was raised from the dead by the Spirit.

It tells us in Romans 6:4 that, "Christ was raised up from the dead by the glory of the Father."

The manifestation of God's glory in the "glorious church" will be a revelation of the Spirit of God in a degree the church has never known.

It will be the third and last great outpouring of the Spirit which the Bible prophesies.

Types and Shadows

The New Testament tells us that God's dealings with the children of Israel were types and figures and "are written for our admonition, upon whom the ends of the world (ages) are come" (1 Corinthians 10:11). (See also v. 6.)

The Amplified Bible translates verse 11 as follows:

1 CORINTHIANS 10:11 (*Amplified*)

11 Now these things befell them by way of a figure—as an example and warning [to us]; they were written to admonish and fit us for right action by good instruction, we in whose days the ages have reached their climax—their consummation and concluding period.

The significance of what God taught the children of Israel about the rains is of utmost importance to we who live in the last of the last days.

Many spiritual Jews have long divided the six-day work week God gave Adam like this (using 1000 years as a day): Two days of chaos. Two days of the law. Two days of Messiah. Then would come the seventh day of rest.

They correctly saw that the Messiah would come after four days—after 4000 years. (They believe that He did not come because they were not ready.) The two days of His rule, being the last of the three periods, were called "the last days."

When Jesus came 2000 years ago, it was the beginning of the last days. We live at the end of the last days.

The Scripture's progressive revelation of the rains is of utmost importance to we who live in the last minutes, if not seconds, of the last days.

The Rains

First mention of the rains occurred when God brought the chosen nation out of Egypt and into the Promised Land.

DEUTERONOMY 11:10,11

10 For the land, whither thou goest in to possess it, is not as the land of Egypt, from whence ye came out, where thou sowedst thy seed, and wateredst it with thy foot, as a garden of herbs:

11 But the land, whither ye go to possess it, is a land of hills and valleys, and drinketh water of the rain of heaven.

Agriculture in Egypt depended upon the rise and fall of the Nile. Irrigation ditches were dug and waterwheels operated with the feet. Harvest in the Promised Land depends upon seasonal rains. Those rains would depend upon their loving and obeying God.

DEUTERONOMY 11:13,14

13 And it shall come to pass, if ye shall hearken diligently unto my commandments which I command you this day, to love the LORD your God, and to serve him with all your heart and with all your soul,

14 That I will give you the rain of your land in his due season, the first rain and the latter rain, that thou mayest gather in thy corn, and thy wine, and thine oil.

Israel has two seasonal rains. The former rains begin in late October and November. They are the first rains of the civil year which begins just before the rains start. The former rains prepare the ground for planting the seed. The latter rains are in late winter and early spring. They water the fields just before the early barley harvest. Without the rains there are no harvests.

DEUTERONOMY 11:16,17

16 Take heed to yourselves, that your heart be not deceived, and ye turn aside, and serve other gods, and worship them;

17 And then the LORD's wrath be kindled against you, and he shut up the heaven, that there be no rain, and that the land yield not her fruit....

God warned Israel against the idolatrous worship of the Canaanites who later tempted them probably saying something like, "Oh, Jehovah was all right down there in Egypt with the Nile and all. But here we must appease our rain god. His name is Baal."

In the progressive revelation of the Bible we see that the rains are heavy with meaning.

God's people were to wait only upon God for the rains. (Jeremiah 14:22.)

God's people were to ask the Lord for the rains. (Zechariah 10:1.)

The Holy Spirit through the prophet Joel reveals that these rains are types and shadows of the outpouring of God's Spirit:

JOEL 2:23-25,28,29

23 Be glad then, ye children of Zion, and rejoice in the LORD your God: for he hath given you the former rain moderately, and he will cause to come down for you the rain, the former rain, and the latter rain in the first month.

24 And the floors shall be full of wheat, and the fats shall overflow with wine and oil.

25 And I will restore to you the years that the locust hath eaten, the cankerworm, and the caterpillar, and the palmerworm....

28 And it shall come to pass afterward, that I will pour out my spirit upon all flesh; and your sons and your daughters shall prophesy, your old men shall dream dreams, your young men shall see visions:

29 And also upon the servants and upon the handmaids in those days will I pour out my spirit.

Peter, preaching on the day of Pentecost revealed that the outpouring of the Holy Spirit was in fulfillment of Joel's prophecy.

ACTS 2:14-18

14 But Peter standing up with the eleven, lifted up his voice, and said unto them, Ye men of Judaea, and all ye that dwell at Jerusalem, be this known unto you, and hearken to my words:

15 For these are not drunken, as ye suppose, seeing it is but the third hour of the day.

16 But this is that which was spoken by the prophet Joel;

17 And it shall come to pass in the last days, saith God, I will pour out of my Spirit upon all flesh; and your sons and your daughters shall prophesy, and your young men shall see visions, and your old men shall dream dreams:

18 And on my servants and on my handmaidens I will pour out in those days of my Spirit; and they shall prophesy.

The outpouring of the Holy Spirit in the book of Acts is the former rain outpouring of the Holy Spirit. It came to prepare the ground for the sowing of the seed.

The latter rain outpouring came at the beginning of this last prophetic century of the sixth day. The Azusa Street outpouring was a part of it. The old-timers we've been referring to were a part of it. It came before the early harvest.

But the Bible prophesies an outpouring when the early rains and the latter rains will come together. Joel prophesied a coming of the former rain and the latter rain in the first month. (Joel 2:23.)

The Holy Spirit through James revealed that the great third and final outpouring of the age will come just before the coming of the Lord!

JAMES 5:7,8

7 Be patient therefore, brethren, unto the coming of the Lord, Behold, the husbandman waiteth for the precious fruit of the earth, and hath long patience for it, until he receive the early and latter rain.

8 Be ye also patient; stablish your hearts: for the coming of the Lord draweth nigh.

The Husbandman is God the Father. (John 15:1.) A husbandman is a farmer. God the Father is the best Farmer ever there was or ever will be. He has a field. Earth. God's field will receive an outpouring of the Spirit likened unto the former and latter rains coming together. The glories of this outpouring will produce the grandest crop ever there was or ever will be. A great harvest of the "precious fruit of the earth" will come in to the glory of God the Father.

The third and last outpouring of the Spirit before Jesus comes will include everything in the book of Acts plus everything in the outpouring at the beginning of this century put together!

Witness the Rains

20

God's call upon my life involves being a "witness." I am to go about the earth and watch what He is doing and tell others. It amazes me how He makes it possible for me to do so.

In 1991 He impressed upon my spirit that I should spend the winter of '91 and '92 in Israel. When I prayed, His direction came to me quite clearly. He wanted me to witness some things which were very big. There would be an element of surprise in it. And He would widen the audience to hear the witness. Perhaps this book is just that.

We live in northeastern Oklahoma near Tulsa. Our finances seemed to say that it would be stretching it to spend the winter in Oklahoma City. But as soon as I made the decision, the money began to pour in to go.

I arrived at my Hebrew school in November. It was cold. And miracle of miracles, it was raining!

Israel had experienced a record drought for the five preceding years. I had been there many times with groups during the drought. I had viewed the Sea of Galilee from high above on the Cliffs of Arbel. The shrinking of the beautiful little sea which is the country's reservoir was unbelievable.

Everyone said the greatest threat to their survival was not war. It was lack of water. Their water supply was disappearing even while their population was swelling. The Russian Jews were coming home in large numbers.

Strict measures were enacted. There were even rules about flushing toilets.

Bright Jews were brainstorming. Bringing in an iceberg was proposed among other desperate measures.

Scientists daily reported on the status of the Sea of Galilee with dire forecasts of just how long they could exist.

Our Jewish friends asked us to pray for rain. Group after group who came with us prayed openly the way we pray and the Jews said, "Amen."

In telephone calls before I came for the winter my friends advised me to bring warm clothes. But I was not prepared. It was so cold I sometimes put on all the clothes I could and stayed in bed under all the covers I could find.

The cold was only surpassed by the rain. It rained and rained and rained. All day. Every day. It rained in sheets. Cold windy sheets.

Newspaper banner headlines in huge type read: NES! NES! NES!

Nes is Hebrew for miracle.

And it was a miracle indeed.

Record snows fell on Mount Hermon. The dews of Hermon literally give the water of life to Israel. (Psalm 133:3.) Snow water runs off to fill three small tributaries which feed the Jordan above the Sea of Galilee.

The Sea of Galilee overflowed its banks. Scientists had predicted it would take years to fill up in normal rainy seasons. The Jordan swelled and rolled, the news reported, "as it must have in Bible days."

Our Hebrew school went to Tiberias to take a look at it. We drove our bus through the flooded streets of the city. They so wanted us to see the miracle, they encouraged us to get out and walk to the banks of the sea where high waves were crashing.

A little Russian Jewish boy—a new immigrant—ran too close to the water's edge. His mother flew after him struggling with her umbrella in the wind. He stopped just in time. But she toppled in. She looked rather like Mary Poppins bobbing up and down in the churning sea hanging on to the umbrella over her head. Of course, someone rescued her from the miracle waters.

Those waters were so powerful and the waves so big they crumpled sidewalks and broke large glass windows in the hotels lining the shores.

Making my way to classes each day was a challenge. I'd seen winds and rains in Oklahoma. But not like that. For they went on day after day after day. One day the winds picked up my umbrella and me with it and flung us face down into the mud. But I was glad. It was miracle mud.

The former rains and latter rains had come heavy—and together! There was no slackening off period between them. October. November. December. January. February. March. It rained. It broke all records!

The Dessert Bloomed

A tour group was to meet me in March. Now they would be witnesses. Not to the rains. They stopped in mid-March. But to their results.

I have ridden many busses through the Land. But never have my eyes beheld what we saw that spring. Bright flowers carpeted the Land of Israel.

The miracle of miracles was the Judean desert. Normally a brown rocky wilderness, it was blanketed with green grasses and red and yellow and purple and blue and whatever color flowers come in. They measured one square meter, and counted the varieties of wild flowers. There were more than twenty. Veteran desert guides said through the media they had never seen the desert like that. *Seed came up they didn't even know was there!*

Prophecy Fulfilled

The Lord drew my attention to two things in this.

First, He told me to read Isaiah 35:1. I had read it many times, "The wilderness and the solitary place shall...blossom as the rose." I'd always interpreted it to mean the things Israel was growing from irrigation in the desert.

But the Lord said to me, "Isaiah didn't write in chapters and verses. Back up to the end of chapter 34 and read it in context."

ISAIAH 34:16,17; 35:1

16 Seek ye out of the book of the LORD, and read: no one of these shall fail, none shall want her mate: for my mouth it hath commanded, and **his spirit it hath gathered them.**

17 And he hath cast the lot for them, and his hand hath divided it unto them by line: **they shall possess it for ever,** from generation to generation shall they dwell therein.

1 **The wilderness and the solitary place shall be glad for them: and the desert shall rejoice, and blossom as the rose.**

I saw it! It's talking about the Ingathering of the Jews! He scattered the Jews in the Diaspora. But the Bible says in many places that just before the Messiah comes He will gather them.

The Berlin Wall fell without the influence of any super power or mighty army. God pushed it down. When it fell, the teeth of Communism were pulled. In 1991 Jews from behind the Iron Curtain came home to Israel in record numbers.

And the desert was blossoming for them!

It was a sign of the coming of the Lord!

So were the rains!

The Lord said to me, "These physical rains in Israel are a sign of what is about to happen in the Church. Israel is prophetic of what is about to occur in the church. Tell them the rains of the Spirit are coming. *And seed is going to come up they didn't even know was in the ground.*"

There is no describing the power and absolute "uncontrollability" of the rains.

Many have seen moves of the Spirit and great revivals. Many have seen the revival of divine healing of the '40s and '50s. But not many remain who have seen an outpouring.

You and I will.

We are in the edges of it now.

Let's examine the earlier outpourings for the place of the Blood.

The Blood and the Outpourings

21

The Old Testament prophesied that three outpourings of the Spirit would come in the last days. Two have been fulfilled.

At the beginning of the last days the Spirit of the Lord was poured out as the book of Acts records: *The Former Rain Outpouring.*

At the beginning of the Twentieth Century—the last century before the millennial change— the second outpouring blessed the earth: *The Latter Rain Outpouring.*

At the end of this prophetic century we are now experiencing showers from the clouds gathered and almost ready to burst forth in the final outpouring of the last days just before the coming of the Lord: *The Former and Latter Rains Together Outpouring.*

First the Blood

There were no outpourings of the Spirit in Old Testament times.

The Spirit was not poured out then because the Blood had not yet been poured out in the earth.

The Spirit goes where the Blood has cleansed.

The Old Testament typifies this when the priest applied the Blood first and then the oil. Oil is a type of the Holy Spirit. (Leviticus 14:14-17.)

A simply profound line in one of Charles Wesley's songs declares, *"His Spirit answers to the blood."*

Every outpouring of the Holy Spirit was and will be in answer to the Blood of Jesus the Messiah.

His Blood was poured out at Calvary so the Spirit could be poured out at Pentecost.

His Blood was magnified in the Holiness movement which went before and prepared the church for the latter rain outpouring at the beginning of this century. And the newly filled saints of the outpouring were taught by the Holy Spirit to honor and give place to the Blood for manifestation of the power of the Spirit.

A great emphasis upon the Blood of Jesus must precede and accompany the fullness of the outpouring of the Spirit which is almost upon us.

The Lord led me to study the outstanding emphasis upon the Blood that went before and was a part of the latter rain outpouring at the beginning of the Twentieth Century. I believe this was so that I could gather some information to share with those who would take part in the last outpouring of the age.

He did this when He gave me a strong desire to know what the old-timers knew about the Blood. For the old-timers we've been talking about were a part of the latter rain outpouring.

The Latter Rain Outpouring

22

B elievers in the early days of the church walked in the power of the outpouring of the Spirit. For a few hundred years they followed the simple teachings of the Master. Then things happened—they would fill several books, but can be reduced to the efforts of the enemy to weaken the body of Christ—which resulted in the church's losing truth and power. The Dark Ages settled upon the world when the light of the gospel was sequestered from common men.

Again, Satan must have thought he'd won. The church could never be glorious as God had said. The glory of God could never again fill the earth as God had said.

But God restored what the cankerworm and the locust had eaten. Vital tenets of the church returned in divine revelations of: The way of salvation—the just shall live by faith. Divine healing. And, at the beginning of this century, the baptism in the Holy Spirit with the initial evidence of speaking in tongues.

On one side of the globe He revealed the baptism in the Holy Spirit in Russia. The thrilling first chapter of Demos Shakarian's book *The Happiest People on Earth* records it.[1]

On this side of the world, just before the century dawned, a desire arose in Reverend Charles Parham's heart: *What exactly does the Bible mean when it speaks of being baptized in the Holy Spirit?*

Miraculously the Lord led him to an overgrown mansion on the outskirts of Topeka, Kansas, where he was to have a Bible school to learn the answer to that question. The students, some sent there quite supernaturally, were encouraged to study the Word independently on the subject. When they met together the consensus was that in the Bible the baptism in the Holy Spirit was evidenced by speaking in tongues.

In a watch night service December 31, 1900, the students waited on the Lord in prayer. A little past midnight 1901, Agnes Ozman was the first to be baptized in the Spirit and speak with other tongues.

The disciples in the Jerusalem outpouring spilled out of the Upper Room into the streets of Jerusalem. The participants at Topeka spilled out of Kansas with news of their blessing. Some stopped off at the Tulsa area and my great-grandparents were a part of the Holy Ghost revival there.

Parham took his Bible school to Houston. There a spiritual black man, William J. Seymour, accepted what Parham taught.

Seymour believed but had not received the experience himself when he was invited to preach at a Holiness church in Los Angeles. After he preached on the baptism in the Holy Ghost and that tongues was the initial evidence, the pastor shut down the meeting and padlocked the door. The tiny congregation accepted the message, however. And Richard and Ruth Asberry invited Seymour and the others to hold prayer meetings in their home at 216 Bonnie Brae Street.

Thomas R. Nickel tells it like this in his book AZUSA STREET OUTPOURING As Told To Me By Those Who Were There:

> Some nights later, on April 6, 1906, Brother Seymour and seven others were seated in the living room, in a spirit of prayer and waiting upon the Lord. Suddenly, as by a bolt of lightning from Heaven, they were all knocked from their chairs to the floor, and many began speaking with other tongues...
>
> Little Willella Asberry rushed from the kitchen to see what was happening in the living room. Young Bud Traynor was on the front

porch, prophesying and preaching. Jennie Moore stood up and prophesied in what the others declared was Hebrew. Then she went to the piano and, for the first time in her life, began playing beautiful music and singing a beautiful language with a beautiful voice. These gifts she never lost...

The news spread like wild-fire. White people joined the colored people, overflowing the house. The front porch became the pulpit and the street became the pews. An old deserted two-story building was located at 312 Azusa Street, a dead-end street only about a half block long...

The great earthquake struck San Francisco and surrounding countryside on April 18. The quake and the disastrous fires that followed took several thousand lives. On the 19th, a lesser shock struck Los Angeles. Many began to seek closer relationship with God.

Ruth Asberry and Jennie Moore went to Peniel Hall... Jennie spoke in tongues, and Ruth explained: "This is that prophesied by Joel." The crowd followed them to Azusa Street, and the great rush was on.

Tent meetings, missions and churches were so emptied that some closed and joined the movement. The upstairs was the tarrying room, but many received their baptism just sitting in the lower services. Joseph Seymour had become a sort of moderator, and he was a marvelous teacher of the deep things of God, though usually he sat with his head bowed inside the shoe-box pulpit, while God carried on the meeting. Only the anointed would preach. As many as nine services were held in one day. The meetings continued day and night, around the clock. People would come in and kneel and pray, then sit with eyes closed and quietly wait for God to work. Two favorite songs were, "Under the Blood" and "The Comforter is Come." Singing in the Spirit, like unto some perfect Heavenly choir, struck awe to all newcomers. Prophecies, messages and interpretations were given with convicting power as though the Lord Himself was speaking directly.

Conversions, the Baptism of the Holy Ghost, miraculous healings, and casting out demons became regular procedures. The power could be felt even five blocks away.[2]

The power resounded around the world.

In 1906, Thomas B. Barrett, a well-known Methodist minister in Oslo, Norway came to the U.S. for other reasons, but was drawn by the power to Azusa Street where he was baptized in the Holy Spirit. He took the message to Norway and became a leader in the establishment of Pentecostal fellowships throughout Europe and the Third World.

English by birth, Barrett visited Alexander Boddy's Anglican church in Sunderland, England, in September, 1907. When "the fire fell," as they described it, several experienced the baptism in the Holy Spirit. Sunderland became the "Azusa" of England and Europe.

In my research, a statement I found in a little book by Donald Gee led me to a treasure trove of information on the latter rain outpouring and the place the Blood held in its manifested power. Gee, a well-respected early Pentecostal pastor, teacher, and author, said that the one who chronicled the outpouring best was Alexander Boddy. He said that the well-educated Boddy did this through his monthly publication *Confidence* (1908-26).

---

[1]Demos Shakarian, *The Happiest People on Earth*, (1975).
[2]Thomas R. Nickel, *AZUSA STREET OUTPOURING As Told To Me By Those Who Were There*, (Great Commission International, Box 1249, Hanford, CA 93230, 1956, 1979).

The Blood and the Latter Rain Outpouring

23

T he copies of *Confidence* I obtained opened a wonderful window for me to watch the outpouring at the turn of the century. Its long issues reported in such detail I felt like a close observer at their meetings. I saw plainly the place of the Blood in the outpouring and in their lives.

Boddy wrote in the first issue, April, 1908, "What hath God wrought? A year ago the writer only knew of some five or six persons in Great Britain who were in the experience. At the time of printing this there are probably more than 500."[1]

The lead article was entitled, "His Own Blood." Boddy opened with this statement, "We praise our God that He is teaching us in these days the wonderful depth, efficacy, and the power of the Blood. This wonderful plan of redemption, which only a God could have conceived and only a God could have carried out, goes to the root of the matter."[2]

Two ladies who were the first to receive at Sunderland wrote their testimony for the first issue:

> God...directed us to come to Sunderland and wait here with His children for our "Pentecost," with signs following. He heard us, and on the night of Sunday, September 1st, 1907, He came "suddenly," as He had promised, and filled these Temples with His glory, simultaneously speaking through us in new Tongues, filling us to the overflow with the joy of His Presence...We entered in through the precious Blood, the only way of perfect cleansing...
>
> (Written seven months since their baptism.) Pentecost has meant for us the Victory of Jesus in the daily life. Victory against the fiercest

onslaughts of Satan. They overcame him by the Blood of the Lamb and the word of their Testimony, and they loved not their lives unto the death.

Margaret E. Howell

Mabel C. Scott[3]

The format of *Confidence* included many reports from across England and around the world. The first issue included a report from Bowland Street Mission in Bradford, England. Its writer would become a regular contributor—as well as one of the most powerful ministers the church has ever known. His name: Smith Wigglesworth.

Wigglesworth received his baptism in the Holy Spirit at Sunderland. Again, you can see the place of the blood in those days in his own account in his biography, *The Apostle of Faith*:

> For four days I wanted nothing but God. But after that, I felt I should leave for my home, and I went to the Episcopal vicarage to say good-bye. I said to Mrs. Boddy, the vicar's wife: "I am going away, but I have not received the tongues yet." She answered, "It is not the tongues you need, but the Baptism." "I have received the Baptism, Sister," I protested, "but I would like to have you lay hands on me before I leave." She laid her hands on me and then had to go out of the room.
>
> The fire fell. It was a wonderful time as I was there with God alone. He bathed me in power. I was conscious of the cleansing of the precious Blood, and I cried out: "Clean! Clean! Clean!" I was filled with the joy of the consciousness of the cleansing. I was given a vision in which I saw the Lord Jesus Christ. I beheld the empty cross, and I saw Him exalted at the right hand of God the Father. I could speak no longer in English but I began to praise Him in other tongues as the Spirit of God gave me utterance. I knew then, although I might have received anointings

previously, that now, at last, I had received the real baptism in the Holy Spirit as they received on the day of Pentecost.[4]

Wigglesworth closed his report from Bradford in the first issue of *Confidence* with a poem. It may have come with his vision. Certainly it was a psalm from His spirit so recently filled to overflowing with the Holy Spirit:

My soul is filled with boundless love
Whilst gazing on the precious blood,
I catch the rays of Jesus' face
Transfixed in me, the Throne of Grace.
Wonders beyond the human mind
Rushing into me, a Life Divine;
I feel the Power of the Holy Dove,
And speak in 'Tongues' of things above.

A. A. Boddy made a trip to Scotland and reported for the first issue on the outpouring there:

The Writer was so overwhelmed by the sights and scenes which met him on some of the last days of March, that he could say, "Behold, the one half was not told me."
...There is great Spiritual Power in the meetings...Scottish people know their Bibles. They are no fools, not carried away easily. But they know that God has appeared in their midst, and they praise Him and they exalt the ever precious BLOOD by which Victory is assured.

Reverend Barratt from Norway traveled extensively and sent reports to *Confidence* from around the world. He signed a letter in the first issue: *Yours for ever in the Blood and Fire—BARRATT.*

The September 1908 issue of *Confidence* was printed one year after "the fire fell" at Sunderland. In the opening article, *"A Year of Blessing. September,*

1907 - September 1908," Boddy enumerated twelve things they were thankful to God for. Here are the first three:

> 1.—No one but the Lord could have given to His servants in this place (and to those who come long distances in order to have fellowship with Him), such real hunger after Himself, such a desire to be loyal to the Lord and to His will.
>
> 2.—We thank Him for the difference, in many ways, between this year and previous years in the matter of Worship.
>
> We have not forgotten that Prayer Meetings before were occasionally successful, though it was very hard to keep them up, they would dwindle and die. But Pentecostal Prayer Meetings (full of power and almost nightly) have gone on all the year round, equally successful in summer and in winter. The Lord makes His presence so real that we cannot stay away. They go on of themselves, for He is present...
>
> 3.—During the past twelve months the Atoning work of God's Incarnate Son has, in a new way, been ever our theme. The precious Blood of the Lord Jesus has been our constant and only plea, and we have, as never before, adored the Lamb that has been slain, worshipping Him in spirit and in truth, and in other tongues as the Spirit Himself gave utterance.[5]

Boddy visited Pastor Polman's work in Amsterdam and wrote an in-depth report of the power of Pentecost in Holland:

> It was a most remarkable meeting as these dear Dutch saints prayed and sang in their own language or in Tongues, and now and again a wave of power would just send them all adoring the Lamb together. When the Blood was honoured the power was greatest.[6]

A letter from Motherwell, Scotland, included in the anniversary issue is very enlightening:

...We were at Kilsyth 10 days ago and had a magnificent time. We had an altar-call on Sabbath evening, and never, even when the work first began here, have we had such power. We just gathered at the front, perhaps three seats full on each side, and began to pray. When the Fire fell the scene and the glory were indescribable.

God means us to go on day by day getting more and more of Himself. Was glad to see your article on "The Pleading of the Blood." "Boldness to enter the Holiest by the Blood."

We got a message last Tuesday, when a few of us gathered for prayer, confirming to us in the fact that "In the pleading of the Blood from the Heart lies your Victory." Then came, "Read Leviticus," so have been going through it again, noting what God hath wrought and the place into which He has magnified the Blood. We are so apt to look at the matter critically, forgetting that, even when we stand at Heaven's gate, we shall have no other plea for entrance but the Precious Blood.

Then there is, perhaps, another reason why, at this time as never before, we need to plead "the Blood." Christian Science, Spiritualism, and even the New Theology is just Christianity without "the Blood," spurious and sham... "The Atonement," as a putting away of sin and sacrifice, is absent from the latter-day counterfeits... Then in Peter's Epistle, the last apostasy is denial of the Lord "that bought them." The purchase of "the Blood."

There seems to be far more truth than we ever dreamt of in the old Hymn, "The Spirit answers to the Blood," sung and experienced by the Wesleyan Methodists in the days when God worked by them and in them....

Victor Wilson

There is not space for more. But I could quote issue after issue of *Confidence* with references to the Blood's part in the Spirit's outpouring.

I could quote issue after issue of *The Pentecostal Evangel,* the Assemblies of God periodical. More often than not the editorial article by Stanley Frodsham (Wigglesworth's friend and biographer) was about the Blood of our redemption.

I found wonderful articles by Lilian B. Yeomans and others still known and revered today who were part of this outpouring.

Now for a brief look at the signs, wonders, and miracles which accompanied the outpouring.

[1] A. A. Boddy, *Confidence,* No. 1, April, 1908, Sunderland.

[2] Ibid. 4.

[3] Ibid. 5.

[4] Stanley Frodsham, *Smith Wigglesworth: Apostle of Faith* (Gospel Publishing House, Springfield, MO 65082), 44.

[5] A. A. Boddy, *Confidence,* No. 6, September 15, 1908, Sunderland, 3,4.

[6] Ibid. 7.

The Anointing for Power 24

ome names held in honor today—Wigglesworth, Lake, Woodworth-
Etter, and many others—received their baptisms in the Holy Spirit in
the latter-rain outpouring.

Ministers have searched for keys to their successes. Miracles and healings
are well documented. People were raised from the dead during their
ministries.

In my study I have come to see how the outpouring of the hour affected
them.

For one thing, when they received the Holy Spirit it was just that—Holy.
Their awe of the God of the anointing never left them.

When the Spirit was poured out, it was a miraculous wonder to them.
They hadn't gotten "used to" tongues and prophecy. They respected the gifts.

It was accepted that to walk in such wondrous and holy things, one would
need to walk cleansed. The blood was for that.

Later, two or three generations or so, outward things were taught for
holiness. But at the first when they spoke of holiness, they spoke of the
Blood.

John G. Lake

John G. Lake sent a report from South Africa to *Confidence* for the
August, 1909 issue:

> The night before last a cripple native woman came to the meeting on her
> hands and knees. She had been in this condition several years. We prayed

for her. Jesus instantly set her free, so she arose and walked, praising God. Several gave their hearts to God at that time. We make them pray through until God fills their souls with Himself. This morning another woman came with violent pains in her head, chest, and back, apparently pneumonia. We prayed for her. Jesus instantly healed her; she burst into tears. The Spirit came upon her, and she was saved right there...

At Potgeitersrust a dead child came back to life when our native evangelist prayed seven hours after it died. At a children's meeting (native children) a choir of angels appeared (angel children), and sang, "Suffer little children to come unto Me." Many dying were healed, and when I went there they came rejoicing to shew me how Jesus had helped them.

Your Brother in Jesus Christ,

John G. Lake

One of the greatest honors of my life began the day an older, gentle couple walked into my office in about 1979. It was John G. Lake's daughter, Gertrude, and her husband Wilford Reidt, a student in Lake's Bible school. We became fast friends. And I observed in them the power of the Spirit of prayer and healing.

The Reidts brought with them a treasure of Lake's sermons and letters. Just recently these were published in a new book: *John G. Lake, His Life, His Sermons, His Boldness of Faith*.[1]

In his sermons it is plain to see that he, like others of the time, was conscious of a Holy Power operating in and through him which he highly respected:

The Baptism of the Holy Ghost is the greatest event in Christian history...Jesus went to the ultimate, to the very Throne and heart of God, and secured right out of the heavenly treasure of the Eternal Soul, the Almighty Spirit, and poured it forth upon the world in divine baptism...the descent of the Holy Ghost brought to the souls of men a UNIVERSAL ministry of Jesus to every man, right from the heart of God. Heavenly contact with the eternal God in power, set their nature all aflame for God and with God, exalted their natures into God, and made the recipient GOD-LIKE. Man became God-like!

Holy Ground

There is no subject in all the Word of God that seems to me should be approached with so much holy reverence, as the subject of the Baptism of the Holy Ghost...

I believe that the first essential in a real Holy Ghost church and a real Holy Ghost work, is to begin to surround the Baptism of the Holy Ghost with that due reverence of God with which an experience so sacred, and that cost such an awful price, should be surrounded.[2]

For this power they respected, the old-timers knew they must be cleansed and the Blood was the only agent. John G. Lake, in whose hands bubonic plague germs died, and in whose ministry there are hundreds of thousands of cases of medically confirmed healings, tells of his steps to operating in the power and the part of the Blood in it:

After seeking God persistently, almost night and day for two months, the Lord baptized me in the Holy Ghost causing me to speak in tongues and magnify God. I had looked for and prayed and coveted the real power of God for the ministry of healing and believed God that when I was baptized in the Holy Ghost that His presence in me through the Spirit would do for the sick the things my heart desired, and which they needed. Instantly upon being baptized in the Spirit I expected to see the sick healed in a greater degree and in larger numbers than I had before known, and, for a time, I seemed to be disappointed.

How little we know of our own relationship to God! How little I knew of my own relationship to Him; for, day by day, for six months following my Baptism in the Holy Ghost the Lord revealed to me many things in my Life where repentance, confession and restitution were necessary, and yet I had repented unto God long ago. Oh! the deep cleansing, the deep revelations of one's own heart by the Holy Ghost. It was indeed as John the Baptist said, "Whose fan is in his hand, and he will thoroughly purge his floor, and gather his wheat into the garner; but he will burn up the chaff with unquenchable fire" (Matthew 3:12).

First, then, I will say the Baptism in the Holy Ghost meant to me a heart searching as I had never before known, with no rest, until in every instance the blood was consciously applied, and my life set free from the particular thing that God had revealed. As I say, this process continued for six months after my Baptism in the Holy Ghost.

Second, a love for mankind such as I had never comprehended took possession of my life...Such love is not human! Such love is only Jesus Himself, who gave His life for others.

After the mighty love, came the renewed, energized power for healing the sick. Oh! what blessed things God has given on this line! What glorious resurrections of the practically dead! Such restorations of the lame and the halt and the blind!

Then came as never before the power to preach the Word of God in demonstration of the Spirit. Oh! the burning fiery messages! Oh, the tender, tender, loving messages! Oh, the deep revelations of wondrous truth by the Holy Ghost!...

Then came the strong, forceful exercise of dominion over devils, to cast them out. Since that time many insane and demon possessed, spirits of insanity, all sorts of unclean demons, have been cast out in the mighty Name of Jesus through the power of the precious blood.

Saints have been led into deeper life in God. Many, many have been baptized in the Holy Ghost and fire. My own ministry was multiplied a hundredfold in the very lives of others to whom God committed this same ministry. Yea, verily the Baptism in the Holy Ghost is to be desired with the whole heart.

Smith Wigglesworth

The reputation of this spiritual giant is widespread till this day. I would like to have included here all the old articles I found actually written by his hand. But an excellent collection of his early articles and sermons in *Confidence* and the *Pentecostal Evangel* and other early Pentecostal periodicals has been put together by Wayne Warner. SMITH WIGGLESWORTH, *The Anointing of His Spirit*, reveals the respect for the power of God common to the old-timers we've been learning from.[3]

Maria Woodworth-Etter

Speaking of miracles! Signs and wonders! No ministry surpassed the supernatural evident in Maria Woodworth-Etter's ministry. People fell out under the power on trains passing through the area where a Woodworth-Etter meeting was in progress.

Lake said, "...There are...people who are born away up in the blessed dominion of God, like our Mother Etter. They have resurrection power."[4]

Sister Etter placed great faith in the blood to prepare the way for the power to work. Her own account of a great meeting in Los Angeles illustrates this:

The world-wide camp meeting was no doubt the largest gathering of baptized saints in these last days. I had...the 10 o'clock meetings, which would have lasted all day and night, for the power of God was poured out so wonderfully, but I had to close at 2 o'clock for other services...

As they led me to the steps that went off the large platform, I stopped and looked at the many hungry, anxious souls; then the power of God came on me, I raised my hands to heaven and stood there, as the Holy Ghost swept over the multitude. I said, the Lord is going to save a lot of you dear people just now. All who want to be saved just now, while I stand here and sprinkle the blood of Jesus on you, by "Living Faith," come forward. There was a rush from all directions to the platform. They began to weep and shout and scores were converted, without getting on their knees, except those who fell down under the Almighty power of God...

Another day as I came off the platform many that could not get near while I was praying for the sick, stood, looking so sad, crowding around me as near as they could, trying to touch my hands or speak. I stopped to look at them. The power fell on me and swept over them. I raised my hands and told them all to look to Jesus, to look up, to lift their hands and faces to God, that I would sprinkle the blood of the Lamb over them, that they would all be healed. Oh, glory to God. The healing power swept over. Many miracles of healings were wrought, people were saved and baptized.

Now, about two years after, in our convention in Los Angeles, I heard many wonderful testimonies of those who were healed... Two marvelous cases said they were healed the day that I was standing on the steps of the platform.[5]

Brother Anderson's Healing

Brother Anderson came from Portland, Oregon...He had blood poisoning and was covered with ugly running and eating sores; some nearly as large as his hand. He was a nervous wreck, and he could not sleep, and it was affecting his brain. He asked me if there was any hope for him, and I told him if he would give his restored life to be used to the glory of God, the Lord would heal him right now.

He said, "I will."

I prayed for his soul and body, and sprinkled the Blood of Jesus all over him, by a living faith. Bless God, the Blood struck in: I laid hands on him and rebuked the poison, and cast out the unclean spirits, and the plague was stayed, and the blood was cleansed.

The power of God struck him, and he fell and lay like a dead man. I left him lying there, but praise the Lord, the next morning his sores were all gone, not even a scar of those rotten sores. His flesh was like a little child's, where great raw sores had been on his hands and arms. All could see that the Lord had wrought a miracle.

This was in Los Angeles, and in our meeting at Long Hill, Connecticut, a while later, a brother rose in the back of the tent (it was Brother Anderson) and he had just arrived on the grounds, he was full of the Holy Ghost; and his face was shining as he told how God had sent him across the continent, to...tell what great things God had done for him...

I heard this brother testify in Chicago and Philadelphia, many months after and he was perfectly healthy, and giving God the glory.[6]

Mrs. Etter included the words to this song in her book published in 1916:

WHERE THE BLOOD CAN HEAL

Do you seek relief for your sin-sick soul?
You to Christ, then, must make appeal.
There's no other one who can make you whole,
You must come where the blood can heal!

REFRAIN

You must come where the blood can heal,
You must come where the blood can heal;
There's no other one who can make you whole,
You must come where the blood can heal!

Vain are all your hopes of another cure,
Be persuaded, you now, to feel,
Help alone, thro' Christ, that you can secure
You must come where the blood can heal!

Other proffered aids can but you deceive,
At your will, unto life, they steal!
You must look to Christ if you'd hope receive,
You must come where the blood can heal!

Hear you not? 'tis there a decoying voice,
Striving ever to quench thy zeal;
Would you from Him turn, refuge safe to find;
You must come where the blood can heal!

If you would arise from your bed of pain,
To the counsel of Christ then kneel,
'Tis prescribed by Him, and your only hope,
You must come where the blood can heal!

---

[1]*JOHN G. LAKE, His Life, His Sermons, His Boldness of Faith*, Kenneth Copeland Publications, Fort Worth, TX 76192-0001.

[2]Ibid., 475,476.

[3]Wayne Warner, SMITH WIGGLESWORTH, *The Anointing of His Spirit* (Vine Books, Servant Publications, Box 8617, Ann Arbor, MI 48107.)

[4]*JOHN G. LAKE, His Life, His Sermons, His Boldness of Faith*, Kenneth Copeland Publications, Fort Worth, TX 76192-0001., Op. Cit., 509.

[5]Maria Woodworth-Etter, *Signs and Wonders* (Harrison House Publishers, P.O. Box 35035, Tulsa, OK 74153) 251, 252.

[6]Ibid., 256, 257.

The Blood and The Last Outpouring

25

The "former and latter rains together" outpouring has begun in the earth. The outpouring which will culminate in the coming of our Lord and Savior Jesus Christ!

Some of the same signs of the outpouring at the beginning of this century are in our midst now.

Joy and holy laughter, for instance.

Here is Wigglesworth's account of what happened from the time he boarded the train to return home to Bradford after having received the baptism in the Holy Spirit at Boddy's place in Sunderland:[1]

> The first thing I did was to telegraph to my home saying, "I have received the baptism in the Holy Ghost and have spoken in tongues." On the train to my home town, the devil began questioning, "Are you going to take this to Bradford?" As regards my feelings at the moment, I had nothing to take, but the just do not live by feelings but by faith. So I shouted out on the railroad coach to everybody's amazement, "Yes, I'm taking it!" A great joy filled me as I made this declaration, but somehow I knew from that moment it would be a great fight all the time.
>
> When I arrived home one of my sons said to me, "Father, have you been speaking in tongues?" I replied, "Yes, George." "Then let's hear you," he said...
>
> My wife said to me, "So you've been speaking with tongues, have you?" I replied, "Yes."
>
> "Well," she said, "I want you to understand that I am as much baptized as you are and I don't speak in tongues."

I saw that the contest was beginning right at home.

"I have been preaching for twenty years," she continued, "and you have sat beside me on the platform, but on Sunday you will preach yourself, and I'll see what there is in it."

She kept her word. On Sunday she took a seat at the back of the building. We had always sat together on the platform until that day. So the contest had begun right in the church.

There were three steps up to the platform, and as I went up those three steps the Lord gave me the passage in Isaiah 61:1, "The Spirit of the Lord God is upon me; because the Lord hath anointed me to preach good tidings unto the meek he hath sent me to bind up the brokenhearted, to proclaim liberty to the captives, and the opening of the prison to them that are bound."

I was no preacher, but hearing the voice of my Lord speaking those words to me, I began. I cannot now remember what I said, but my wife was terribly disturbed. The bench on which she sat would seat nine people and she moved about on it until she had sat on every part of it. Then she said in a voice that all around her could hear, "That's not my Smith, Lord, that's not my Smith!"

I was giving out the last hymn when the secretary of the mission stood up and said, "I want what our leader has received."

The strange thing was that when he was about to sit down he missed his seat and went right down on the floor. Then my oldest son arose and said he wanted what his father had, and he, too, took his seat right down on the floor. In a short while there were eleven people right on the floor of that mission. The strangest thing was that they were all laughing in the Spirit and laughing at one another. The Lord had really turned again the captivity of Zion and the mouth of His children was being filled with laughter according to the word of the Lord in Psalm 126:1,2.

God said of the deliverance of Israel out of Egypt, "He brought forth His people with joy and His chosen with gladness" (Psalm 105:43). He's about to take His church out of earth and He will bring us out with joy and gladness.

A century, as God sees time—a thousand years is as a day—is only about 2.4 hours. In this prophetic century God has given out the trumpet call, "Jesus is coming soon!"

The outpourings of His Spirit are marked by joy.

For in His Presence is fullness of joy. (Psalm 16:11.)

He will go out to meet the rejoicing ones. (Isaiah 64:5.)

A mark of the previous outpourings has been Pentecostal joy.

Here are a few remarks from various issues of *Confidence*:

> Here were we gathered in an Established Church Vestry, and more talking in Tongues, laughter, and joyful song have we not heard...A large part of the meetings was spent on our knees, praying, singing, or in silence...

> Two manifestations often mark the meetings, "holy laughter," and a "holy hush."

> It was a time of real joy. The radiant, happy faces cheered up everyone. There was infectious joy—the joy of the Lord; even at times there was good-natured, hearty laughter, such as did us all good. There is a time for everything.
> But it was also a solemn time. Jesus Himself stood in our midst and spoke to us, and we were awed and bowed down to the very dust. He was teaching us. He was manifesting His gifts and showing us how to prove all things, how to trust Him, and how to stand on His promises. *The Lord was our Leader.*

The former and latter rain outpouring is upon us.

These are the last of the last days.

We must make much of the Blood for two purposes. To overcome Satan in his endtime wrath. But much more importantly, to prepare us for God's Glory in His endtime revelation through His Glorious Church.

I have included so much from witnesses of the outpouring at the beginning of the century. This is because these old-timers understood truth about the blood and the power which somehow slipped away. It must return for the greater outpouring we are about to know at the end of the century.

I believe we need to return singing about the Blood. Real singing to give the Blood its place in our approach to God. Not merely to singing just a token song in a service, but to singing a while in honor of the Blood. The old-timers said that when they sang about the Blood for a while "a cleansing wave" seemed to sweep over them preceding a wave of the Spirit in power.

The Spirit answers to the Blood.

The Spirit of Glory must complete our preparation now for the Lord of Glory!

Full Circle

It won't be long now until we complete the circle... We are about to return to the fullness of the Glory of the Father's Presence.

Oh! What a Planner! Oh! What a Plan!

Thank God for the Blood and the Glory!

---

[1]Stanley Frodsham, *Smith Wigglesworth: Apostle of Faith* (Gospel Publishing House, Springfield, MO 65082.)

Billye Brim was born again at the age of eight in 1947 and was brought up to love God and His Word. After her initial infilling of the Holy Spirit in 1967, she began the journey of fulfilling the call of God on her life.

Billye served as editor of publications for Kenneth Hagin Ministries from 1970 to 1980, as well as editing books for several other well-known Bible teachers including Dr. Lester Sumrall. In 1972 she began ministering regularly at her local church in Collinsville, Oklahoma. In 1980 she began traveling full time both nationally and internationally, with her focal points in Scandinavia and Europe. She has also ministered seven times in the Soviet Union.

After the homegoing of her husband in 1986, the Lord led Billye to study Hebrew in Israel. Working primarily through a Jewish ulpan (special language school), she takes Christians to Israel at least twice a year to see modern-day Israel through Jewish eyes. Bible prophecy is an important part of Billye's teaching. Billye is a frequent conference speaker (numerous times at Brother Kenneth Copeland's Believers Conventions) and ministers in churches, Bible schools, family camps, and on television. The emphasis of her ministry is on the Glory of God and His Glorious Church. She truly loves the Body of Christ and desires to see it become the Glorious Church Jesus promised to receive unto Himself.

To contact the author, write:
Billye Brim • P.O. Box 126
Collinsville, Oklahoma 74021

Prayer of Salvation

A born-again, committed relationship with God is the key to the victorious life. Jesus, the Son of God laid down His life and rose again so that we could spend eternity with Him in heaven and experience His absolute best on earth. The Bible says, **"For God so loved the world, that he gave his only begotten Son, that whosoever believeth in him should not perish, but have everlasting life"** (John 3:16).

It is the will of God that everyone receive eternal salvation. The way to receive this salvation is to call upon the name of Jesus and confess Him as your Lord. The Bible says, **"That if thou shalt confess with thy mouth the Lord Jesus, and shalt believe in thine heart that God hath raised him from the dead, thou shalt be saved. For whosoever shall call upon the name of the Lord shall be saved"** (Romans 10:9-10,13).

Jesus has given salvation, healing and countless benefits to all who call upon His name. These benefits can be yours if you receive Him into your heart by praying this prayer:

Heavenly Father, I come to You admitting that I am a sinner. Right now, I choose to turn away from sin, and I ask You to cleanse me of all unrighteousness. I believe that Your Son, Jesus died on the cross to take away my sins. I also believe that He rose again from the dead so that I might be justified and made righteous through faith in Him. I call upon the name of Jesus Christ to be the Savior and Lord of my life. Jesus, I choose to follow You, and ask that You fill me with the power of the Holy Spirit. I declare that right now, I am a born-again child of God. I am free from sin, and full of the righteousness of God. I am saved in Jesus' name, Amen.

If you have prayed this prayer to receive Jesus Christ as your Savior, or if this book has changed your life, we would like to hear from you. Please write us at:

Harrison House Publishers

P.O. Box 35035 • Tulsa, Oklahoma 74153

You can also visit us on the web at **www.harrisonhouse.com**

Additional copies of this book are available
from your local bookstore.

Harrison House
Tulsa, Oklahoma 74153

The Harrison House Vision

Proclaiming the truth and the power
Of the Gospel of Jesus Christ
With excellence;

Challenging Christians to
Live victoriously,
Grow spiritually,
Know God intimately.